IF IT WEREN'T
FOR US
CHRISTIANS

THERE'd bE A loT moRE ChRisTiANS

"Email bobby your personal example of how us Christians have scared off potential new Christians. He might include it in his next book (the sequel) and give you the credit you deserve. You will be famous!"

His email address is:

bobby@THECROSSREFERENCE.COM

IF IT WEREN'T FOR US CHRISTIANS

There'd be a lot more Christians

BOBBY WEAVER

If It Weren't For Us Christians
There'd Be A Lot More Christians

BY: BOBBY WEAVER

Published by Crossover Publications LLC, 870 N. Bierdeman Road, Pearl, Mississippi 39208, www.crossoverpublications.com
(601) 664-6717, Fax: (601) 664-6818
Randall M. Mooney
Publisher

Library of Congress Control Number: 2010936753

ISBN 978-0-9819657-6-5
Printed in the USA

Christian Inspirational
Humorous
Non-Fiction

Cover Concept & Direction: Randall M. Mooney
Graphic Arts & Layout: Steve Tadlock
Background Images: 123RF.COM

Acknowledgements

"The following people (and especially God) are the reasons this book exists."
bobby weaver

†   God...for digging me out of the sewer.
†   Randy McInvale...for assisting the Holy Spirit in leading me to Christ. They don't come any more obedient than Randy!
†   Robert P. & Margaret Weaver...my world-class Christian parents.
†   Rev. Ken Taylor...for putting up with that Beach Bull guy.
†   Rev. Don Woolley...for scamming me into leading an Alpha class.
†   Rev. Michael Bryan...for giving me the "rock."
†   Rev. John Friedman...for not kicking the "Rabbi" out of Forest Park United Methodist Church.
†   Rev. Kevin Stewart...for asking me "the question" that saved my life. The boy also taught me how to smoke a mean chicken!
†   Rev. Tom Tillery...for being my Sunday night inspiration.
†   Rev. Bill Small...some call him the "hardest worker" in the UMC.
†   The congregation at Forest Park United Methodist Church, Panama City, FL, and our awesome secretary, Faith Williams.
†   Wendy "Montana" Mohler...for being my Princeton cheerleader.
†   Laura Taylor..."if God can part the Red Sea, he can find a man for me." Go ahead girl, write the book!
†   Mr. Terry Burns...the best Christian literary agent in America.
†   Mr. Randall Mooney...a publisher willing to roll the dice on this book.
†   Vicki Weaver...talking about my girl...thankfully, our divorce just didn't work out.
†   Marlenna Weaver...my oldest and favorite daughter.
†   Brandy Weaver...my middle and favorite daughter.
†   Danielle Weaver...my youngest and favorite daughter.
†   Robert Bakke...my Minnesota motivation, charter jet pilot (Cessna Citation), world-class public speaker and author!
†   Howard Stern...yeah, that Howard Stern...God used him!!!!
†   Mike Seamon and George Stewart..."blue collar Christians for sure!" and you can add Bob & Nancy Berdanier to that list.
†   Scott Tolbert and the Moon-Finger Small Group.
†   The Fishes & Loaves Ministry...thanks to Christina Berry & Michael Hunter, with lots of help from Barney & Marilyn Barnett.
†   The Emmaus Walk 190, Blue Lake, Feb.2008, Table of Paul.
†   Dan Lowe...Dan worships God in a refrigerator...aka Canada.
†   The Characters for Christ small group.

Table of Contents

Chapter One

"Church Nazis"

THE BLATANT:

✝   A Baptist pastor in North Carolina leads his congregation to vote nine members out of the church. Their crime? They supported John Kerry in the 2004 presidential election. The national media has a field day.

✝   Two competing churches in Northwest Florida put up opposing billboards. One declares, *"There ain't no hell!"* The other counters with, *"The hell there ain't!"*

✝   A famous television evangelist is targeted in a prime-time documentary as he globe trots around the world, lavishly spending more in *twenty-four hours* than most of his constituents make in *twenty-four months*.

THE DISCREET:

† A salesman walks into the corporate offices of an insurance company. He informs the secretary that he has an appointment with Mr. Watson, who is a rather high-profile Christian in the local business community. While standing there, he happens to notice Mr. Watson walking down a hallway towards the restroom. The secretary writes down the salesman's name and proceeds to take it back to Mr. Watson's office to see if he is available. A moment later she returns and informs the visitor, "I must have forgotten, Mr. Watson is out of town this week." I know this story is factual because the salesman was none other than yours truly.

† The brand new Cadillac parks in the handicapped space nearest to the front door of Wal-Mart. A young woman gets out and hurriedly runs inside, her Christian t-shirt admonishing readers to "repent while there is still time!" Ted, whose mom is handicapped, observes the woman taking his parking spot. He detests it when people who are obviously not handicapped use those designated parking spaces...another notch in his "excuses for not considering Christianity" belt. Cha-ching!

† A newly ordained minister tells the attendees at a funeral, "John has gone home to be with the Lord." One of the attendees was Tad, a skeptic who had recently started attending church. At least he was seeking. But he knew the deceased well. As the two had recently discussed, John had never accepted Christ and had indicated no intention of doing so. But according to this clergyman, John was now in heaven. "If there is a heaven and John is now there," he reasoned, "I will certainly be there someday. After all, I am a much better person than he was. So why do I need church?" And thanks in part to the minister's words spoken during the service that day, it was the last time Tad ever stepped foot in church.

†

These are just a few actual examples that have led me to believe that some of us must interpret the Great Commission something like this: "Go into the world and scare off as many people from the Christian faith as we possibly can." Let's face it, fellow brothers and sisters in Christ, when it comes to spreading the Gospel, we are often our own worst enemy. I am reminded of a joke that pretty much sums up the way we are often looked at from the secular world's point of view—*a stressed-out woman on a busy boulevard was tailgating a man. Suddenly, the light turned yellow in front of him. He did the right thing, stopping at the crosswalk even though he could have beaten the red light by accelerating through the intersection. The tailgating woman hit the roof, and the horn, screaming in frustration as she missed her chance to get through the intersection with him. As she was still ranting and raving she heard a tap on her window and looked up into the face of a very serious police officer. The officer ordered her to exit the car with arms in the air and then handcuffed her. He escorted her to the police station where she was searched, fingerprinted, photographed and placed in a cell.*

A couple of hours later she was taken back to the booking desk where the arresting officer was waiting with her personal effects. He apologetically explained, "I am very sorry for this mistake."

"How could this possibly have happened?" she demanded.

"Well," he began, "when I pulled up behind your car you were blowing your horn, flipping off the driver and appeared to be cussing a blue streak. I then noticed the 'Choose Life' license plate, the 'What Would Jesus Do?' bumper sticker, the 'Follow Me To Sunday School' decal and the chrome-plated Christian fish emblem on the back of your vehicle. Naturally, I assumed the car was stolen."

Funny, huh? But a lot of times, it's not a joke. Yes, just as our aforementioned police officer had a rather unfortunate encounter with one of us Christians in a fictional setting, many in the secular world have also had their "unfortunate encounter" with one of us in a real-life setting, an encounter that some will remember and quite possibly use against Christianity for the rest of their lives.

Take Cheryl Gibson, for instance. First a little background: In 2002, my wife Vicki and I were asked by our church, Forest Park United Methodist in Panama City, Florida, to lead an Alpha class. Alpha is a rather innovative way to connect with the un-churched and unsaved. I was picked as a leader because of my checkered past. Let me explain. Before accepting Christ on February 26, 1997, at 10:33 a.m. (like anybody's counting), I published one of the most disgusting newspapers in the nation. It was a national chain called *Beach Bull*. The *Bull* contained risqué jokes and scantily clad women in string bikinis. But as God often does, he used my past to enable me to know and relate to the secular society. They had been my customers. I had been their hero…a *role model*, of sorts.

Now I was inviting them to an Alpha class. At this class we invited the skeptics, the atheists, the agnostics, the seekers, our neighbors and family…basically anyone that is either *un-churched* or *unsaved*. Yes, anybody that wants a free, world-class meal; anybody that wants to tell a dirty joke; or anybody that wants to vent about all of us hypocrites in the church. It doesn't sound too churchy, huh? Well, that's because it isn't.

I remember the night of our first Alpha class. We had about twenty-five participants. Some of them came willingly and some had been tricked into thinking it was just a backyard cookout. Cheryl assumed she was attending a barbeque.

As folks began arriving, I remember Dave out back talking to another guest. A used-car salesman and self-professed shade-tree mechanic, he was attending as a result of one of my scams. I told him that he was invited to set us Christians straight…being the big bunch of hypocrites that we were. He couldn't wait!

Soon after Dave arrived, he began telling some guy one of the most expletive-filled jokes I had ever heard. I'll always remember what happened next. When he finished the joke, he introduced himself. "By the way, my name is Dave Rich; what is your name and what do you do?" The guy answered, "My name is Don Woolley, I'm the pastor." The look on Dave's face was classic, a nice shade of red with just a touch of green. Fortunately, someone yelled it was time to eat and Dave ducked for cover.

Anyway, back to my story. As we do in every Alpha class, we went around the room and asked our guests what they thought about the church. Almost to a person, there was one horror story after another. The most memorable was from Cheryl Gibson, the gal who thought she was attending just your basic, run-of-the-mill backyard barbeque. When it came her turn to vent, she told us the story of what she called the *"church Nazis,"* her name for a certain type of supposedly religious people. (By the way, I must thank Ed & Bev Wells for inviting Cheryl to the Alpha class. Her story about the "church Nazis" was the original inspiration for this book).

Church Nazis, according to Cheryl, are those folks that have a "holier than thou" type attitude. If we aren't dressed right, they give us a stare. If we don't know that the book of *Carnations* is actually the book of *Corinthians*, they roll their eyes. If we drive up in a beat up old 1979 Chevy Vega they snicker at us. And if we don't know all the words to *How Great Thou Art,* we are obviously going to hell. And then, at the "meet and greet" part of the church service, if we're not part of the clique, we might as well be invisible. Her exact words escape me but they went something to the effect of: "There were more cliques in the church than in my high school." She was also told that she didn't know how to pray. Funny, I never knew there were rules for prayer etiquette. *Rule #314: Never end a prayer with a preposition!* I must have missed that one.

There is, however, a happy ending to this story. Several of the Alpha class members ended up accepting Christ and getting baptized in the Gulf of Mexico. And about two months later Cheryl, our Church Nazi Mama, began teaching a Sunday school class at our church. Thank the Lord she didn't still drive up in that hideous old '79 Chevy Vega! And, oh yeah, let's not forget Dave, the "expletive not deleted" joke teller. He and his wife, Kathy, joined our church and Dave became head of the Outreach Ministry.

Does God work in mysterious ways or what?

Discussion Guide

1.   God has a specific purpose for each individual on earth. However, we all share one common purpose. What is it?

_____

_____

_____

Hint: Matthew 28:19. Some of us, on the other hand, evidently interpret the Great Commission like this: "*Go into the world and scare off as many people from the Christian faith as we possibly can.*" If you agree, why do you think that is?

_____

_____

_____

2.   Call someone you know that does not go to church. Explain that your group is involved in a study and would like to know if they would assist by answering one question. If they agree, simply ask: "*If you had to describe the church in a sentence or two, what would you say?*" Share their answer with the study group:

_____

_____

_____

3.   It has been said that a certain percentage of people in a typical Sunday morning congregation may be simply "going through the motions" of church. If you happen to agree with that notion and had to guess the percentage of people that fall into

that category, what % would you pick? _____ If you would like, please share with the group why you chose that number:

_____

_____

_____

4. Do you know anyone who says the church has hurt them? _____ In what way were they hurt?

_____

_____

_____

Did this cause them to stop attending church? _____ If so, what might be done to get them to return?

_____

_____

_____

Notes:

Chapter Two

French Buts

I used to teach sailors how to cuss. Think about it. Air Force pilots must be given flying lessons; Marines have to be taught how to kill; Army soldiers must learn to dig foxholes; and Coast Guard folks need to learn how to swim. So naturally, Navy sailors must perfect the art of cussing. Besides, it comes in handy when you drop a 400-pound boat anchor on your foot. (Hey, Navy people, I'm just kidding. Smiley face goes here).

The true test of one's swearing ability is the length of the oath. If we can curse for forty-five seconds or more without using the same cuss-word twice, we're good. I was the best, well almost. I once let out a *two-minute, fifty-second* oath, a personal best that still stands today. But some guy that lives in New Jersey holds the world record. He attempted and beat the 3-minute oath with a world-record time of *three-minutes, seven seconds*. He must have been an admiral or something.

Then a guy named Jesus showed up—new life, new set of values. I was taught that in Ephesians 4:29, Paul tells us not to let any unwholesome talk come out of our mouths. He must not have been much of a sailor. I mean really! If Paul had been proficient at swearing, he might have avoided a shipwreck or two? "Look! There's a $%&!!$ rock off the starboard bow. Let's get the !?&%$ out of here!" Surely that would have helped.

Evidently, a lot of us Christians believe that an occasional "bad word" is necessary. And the beautiful part is, we have discovered a little disclaimer that makes it okay. Ever heard it? I'm betting most of us have! Right before we cuss, some of us dismiss our little indiscretion by opening with four seemingly innocent words "Pardon my French but..." It's sort of an unwritten rule that states: "I'm going to sin but this one doesn't count."

"Pardon my French but..." works especially good on those fairly innocuous cuss words, but what about the "real" hardcore profanity? We're talking about those heavy-duty four-letter words, the ones we only say when we hit our thumb with a hammer or when our Sunday school teacher has already left the room.

To help us understand, let's look up "cussing" in the dictionary. Webster defines it as: "using offensive language." Christians aren't supposed to use offensive language; so naturally, we have adopted more "politically correct" cuss-words. Actually, I call this "religiously correct" profanity.

For instance, we all know that a Christian would never use the f-word, right? Well, not exactly. The f-word is such an all purpose expletive that even some of us Christians feel a need to use it as we wind our way through the f-word situations of life. No problem, we have borrowed several synonyms from the secular word and they seem to work just fine. Words like: *frigging, freaking* and *fricking.*

I bet most of us have heard a Christian say something like: "If John isn't careful, he's going to break his freaking neck." Ring a bell? Sure it does, more than likely we hear it several times a week, maybe even in an occasional sermon. But what does this "religiously correct" statement say about us Christians to the secular world, the world we are suppose to be witnessing to?

Or perhaps more importantly, what does it say to our fellow Christians, especially new believers who look to us as role models and for guidance? Here is what it says to me. It says, "We suck!" When I became a Christian, giving up profanity was relatively easy for me...or so I thought. I still cussed but I just used generic terms to make me feel better about myself. I think it was a macho thing. However, while writing this book I decided to give up any and all profane language whatsoever, and that included using the word *suck*. I looked it up in Webster...to suck means to "inhale very rapidly."

And speaking of this famous s-word, it has become so ingrained in our society that even some members of the clergy use it. Occasionally even Spirit-filled Christians use it. Evidently, we either don't know the origin or we don't care. The word *suck*, or *sux* if we're trying to disguise it, was popularized in the Sixties when most of us first heard about alternative lifestyles. Yes, in certain instances, the word has a sexual connotation.

So, what is my point? Good question. I'm glad you asked. My point is that if it weren't for us Christians (and the way we conduct ourselves), there'd be a lot more Christians. No wonder the secular world has a hard time telling us apart from just your basic, run-of-the-mill heathens. So here's the bottom line: if we act like the secular world, look like the secular world, and talk like the secular world, when we finally do get around to witnessing to someone about Christ, we have zero credibility. And pardon my French, but that *inhales very rapidly!*

Discussion Guide

1.　　　There are many admonitions in the Bible concerning the use of profane/unwholesome language. Find and read one scripture that deals with this issue. This scripture can be found in: _____ However, there is one scripture that literally knocks it out of the park. Hint: It can be found in the first chapter of James. What does it say?

2. Do you actually think a few profane words used in front of a non-believer could hurt your Christian witness? _____ Why or why not?

3. Why do you think some of us Christians find it necessary to use profanity (best answer wins a cookie)?

If your brother or sister in Christ uses offensive language in front of you, should you ignore it so as not to cause a confrontation? _____ Why or why not?

4. How many times in a month might you hear someone say, "*Pardon my French, but...?*" _____ Do you think that some of us feel that by using this little disclaimer, it "gets us off the hook" so to speak? _____ Please elaborate:

5. One theory is that some Christian men use profanity to maintain their macho image and not be viewed as a "Christian softie." Do you think there is any credibility to that theory? If so, why?

6. Has this discussion caused you to re-evaluate your own language habits? (No public answer is necessary)
Notes:

Chapter

Three

The "Fish Sign" Warning

My dad was probably the best driver that ever lived. My mom was probably the worst driver that ever lived. I remember the day in 1954 when my dad was teaching my mom how to drive. She took her best shot at killing the entire family. Fortunately, Daddy grabbed hold of the steering wheel at the last possible second and an imminent head-on collision was avoided by a gnat's eyebrow. That was the first and last time my mom ever drove. There is a God!

I still remember the absolute terror to this day. I was horrified. It left an indelible impression on me. Thanks to my dad's teaching and my mom's attempt at vehicular homicide, I consider myself a very safe driver. And I hate to admit this, but I am now almost obsessed with the driving skills, or lack thereof, of other drivers. And less than perfect drivers really did not want to cross paths with me during my pre-Jesus days.

Here's a for instance…but first a question: what is the number one cause of wrecks in America today? What's your guess; reckless driving, drunk driving, driving too fast, driving too slowly? None of the above, the correct answer is *tailgating*. Yes, and here's the bummer, most of us tailgate! That's right, seventy-five percent of all drivers in America tailgate. By the way, if you're one of the twenty-five percent that don't, please accept my apologies.

Now, back to my story. Most folks love to wake up in the morning to the aroma of roasting coffee. I used to love to wake up to the aroma of *roasting rubber*...as in slammed on brakes. That's right; I would get in my vehicle and time it just right so that I would end up immediately in front of a female driver. I chose women because I could out-run most of them up if a fight ensued. Invariably, the driver would get right on my rear bumper. And then, when she least expected it, I would hit the brakes...hard! Can you say *road rage*? I knew you could.

Now, here is the truth: I'm not proud of any of what I just admitted, but it's the truth. Thank God for forgiveness or this boy would be up the creek without a trolling motor. It was February 26, 1997, when I let go and let God. I had done a fine job of ruining my life and decided to give God a shot. My road rage was one of God's biggest challenges. I wasn't real sure he was up to the task. He was, but I went down kicking and screaming all the way.

That was then, this is now. I finally gave it up. In fact, along the way I invented a game to help me deal with this sickness. Now every time I see someone driving less than perfect, instead of waving the "you're number one" finger at him or her, I just think of a blessing that God has given me. For instance, when I see a person fail to use their turn signal, instead of condemning their entire existence, I think of a blessing...like maybe the little insignificant time when God healed my daughter from a massive brain tumor. Yeah, when we start concentrating on God's blessings in our life, we might find ourselves like I did...actually hoping a driver would do something dumb. Then we get to remember another blessing. Try it, I promise it works.

So, what does the fish sign have to do with all this? Everything...let me explain. First, let me say that I think we should all be proud of our faith and displaying Christian bumper stickers or whatever can be a wonderful thing. However, I also think most of us would agree that as Christians, we should be the most careful, courteous drivers on the road. But a few of us aren't. I don't know if it's because when we're tooling down the highway we are praying, singing praise and worship tunes, counting our blessings or what. Whatever the reason, a small percentage of us Christian drivers are a touch on the discourteous side, if not downright dangerous.

But here's the kicker, we wouldn't stand out in the crowd as any worse than any of the other drivers except for the fact that some of us that aren't good drivers ADVERTISE IT! Excuse me! We do what? Yes, we put a warning sign on the back of our vehicle that basically says: "Look! I'm a Christian and I may not have any driving manners, so watch out!" The warning comes in the form of that little "fish" emblem (or other Christian stickers and emblems) that we are all familiar with. Believe me, every time we get behind the wheel, many in the secular world put us on trial…and unfortunately, some of us are guilty as charged. So please, for those of us out there who aren't extraordinarily safe and courteous drivers, for goodness sake, let's lose the fish.

Here's a true story: we were talking about Christian behavior in Sunday school one week, and this friend, who shall remain nameless, tells us about an incident that happened as he was driving to work. When he arrived, a driver who had been following him pulls up behind him and yells: "Thanks for cutting me off…Christian!" If this irate guy was looking for an excuse to pass on Christianity, our Christian driver just delivered him one on a silver platter.

Now, some of us might say, "But that's a pretty lame excuse!" Hello, folks, the lamer the better! People who are looking for an excuse don't sit down and evaluate their excuses and then say to themselves, "Well, I doubt if God will buy the bad driver excuse, I better go with either the 'I'm a good person' or the old stand-by, 'I can't stand the hypocrites,' excuse—surely he will bite on one of those!"

And now, as Paul Harvey used to say, here is the rest of the story. The bad driver in this case was none other than a

Sunday school teacher. By the way, he's as genuine a Christian as they come. And yes, he had the "fish warning" sign right on the back of his vehicle. But after he gets through suing me for putting his story in this book, I bet he will become one of the best Christian drivers out there. Hey, maybe this journalistic endeavor will be worth the effort after all.

Discussion Guide

1.   Case Study: You are waiting to pull out onto a main street when you observe a car running the traffic light at least two or three seconds after it had turned red. The violating car narrowly misses hitting another vehicle that had pulled out onto the street after his or her light had turned green. As it turns out, about a block later you find yourself stopped next to the offending driver at another traffic light. The driver has a Christian bumper sticker. His (or her) window is rolled down. Should you very politely make a comment concerning the fact that they almost caused a potentially terrible accident? _____ If so, what might you say?

_____

_____

_____

If not, why?

_____

_____

_____

Should Christians ever get involved in such incidences? _____
Please elaborate:

_____

_____

_____

2.   Within the last month, have you had an "incident" on the road that caused you to become irritated with another driver, or vice versa? _____ If you would like, please share with the group:

_____

_____

_____

Do you feel happy with the outcome, or do you feel that you or the other driver could have handled the situation better? _____
Please elaborate:

_____

_____

_____

3.   Do you agree with the notion that Christian drivers should be the most careful and courteous drivers on the road...and even more so if they display Christian emblems on their vehicles? _____
Please elaborate:

_____

_____

_____

4.   Case Study: Every Sunday at your church one particular family always parks near the front entrance. The driver invariably pulls into the space at an angle that eliminates the possibility of another vehicle parking in the adjoining space. You happen to be walking by one Sunday morning when once again, the driver takes up one and a half spaces. This is typically where elderly members of the church park because of its close proximity to the sanctuary entrance. Should you point out the problem to the driver? _____ If so, how would you handle it?

_____

_____

_____

If not, why?

_____

_____

_____

5.   Do you think that if a Christian is less than an exemplary driver, he or she should consider not displaying Christian bumpers stickers, decals and emblems on their vehicle? _____ Please make a case for your answer:

_____

_____

_____

6.   Do you think it is possible for a non-believer to use someone's bad driving as just another excuse to shun Christianity? _____
Please explain:

_____

_____

_____

7.   In your opinion, what driving habit on American highways causes the most accidents?

_____

_____

_____

According to most law enforcement agencies, the answer is *tailgating*. Hint: Put 3 car lengths per 10 MPH between you and the vehicle in front of you and don't worry about it.

CHAPTER

FOUR

Feathers

If we go to church on a regular basis, I bet we can count on just one thumb all the sermons we've heard on the topic of *gossip*. In fact, even if both of our thumbs have been cut off we could probably still count them. Why is that? I suspect it might be because most of us, including the clergy, *do* **occasionally** gossip. Think about it.

On the other hand, how many sermons have we heard concerning alcohol or drug abuse? We would probably need a lot more thumbs to count the number of sermons which have touched on these subjects. Why is that? I suspect it might be because most of us, including the clergy, *do not* abuse drugs or alcohol.

Do we see a pattern here? It would appear that we prefer to talk about, or preach about, stuff that we or our congregations aren't generally guilty of. That's because we can step on just so many toes before those toes start leading members of the congregation to other churches. How many people in any given church congregation abuse alcohol? My guess is maybe ten percent. So naturally, we hear sermons on the damage caused by drinking. Here's another question: how many people in any given church congregation occasionally gossip? My guess is that the percentage is fairly substantial. Therefore, we probably don't hear too many sermons on the damage caused by gossiping.

Houston, we have a problem!

Okay, so it's Monday morning and time to go witnessing to the secular heathens in that target rich environment, the American workplace. And sure enough, at the office water fountain we might hear the first witnessing line of the day. "Hey Sally, I heard that Mr. Wilson got tanked again this weekend. And I'm betting he flirted with every waitress in the restaurant. Wilson needs to bring his rear end to church!" And guess what Sally is thinking..."Why don't YOU just shut your mouth and learn to quit gossiping, you self-righteous hypocrite?"

Beautiful! We have just managed to scare off another one. I can just see Jesus wiping his brow and saying to himself, "Why in the name of heaven did we ever give them *mouths*?"

Now, I would hope that a greater percentage of Christians don't gossip, but we are going to have a little paper sermon about the "g-word" just in case. The best definition of gossip I've ever heard goes something like this: when we are talking about someone that has done something that we don't agree with, if we are neither part of the *problem* nor part of the *solution*, we are gossiping. Now, here comes the sermon...please turn off your cell phones and get them babies to quit screaming.

A LITTLE PAPER SERMON:

A pastor in a small Southern Baptist church finally decided it was time to confront Ms. Willis about her gossiping. Numerous members had complained about her spreading half-truths and innuendos among the congregation. Pastor Rick decided to begin their discussion by giving her an example of that which he had first-hand knowledge. It was her account of what happened when Chuck Riley left his pick-up truck parked in front of Widow Mary Watson's house over the weekend.

Ms. Willis suspected an affair. And she made sure just about everybody in town knew it. The fact of the matter was, however, that Chuck's truck had broken down on Friday afternoon after an air-conditioning service call. The widow, who also happened to be Pastor Rick's sister, left town five days ago and had asked Rick to call Chuck's Heating and Air-Conditioning to see if he would stop by her house and check on a malfunctioning thermostat.

When confronted by Pastor Rick with those facts, Ms. Willis' face turned a bright shade of red. But he wasn't finished, he wanted to make a point, and boy did he ever! Pastor Rick told Ms. Willis that he wanted her to conduct a special training exercise that might have a rather substantial impact on her life. He handed her a pair of scissors, a pillow and asked her to cut it open. The pillow was full of feathers. Evidently, it wasn't one of the two-dollar pillows from Wal-Mart. Next, Pastor Rick gave her the following instructions: "I want you to spend the next week walking throughout our community placing a feather on every doorstep in town. Don't report back to me until every last doorstep has a feather laying on it." In her humiliation, she agreed to the task.

Ten days later a tired and scruffy Ms. Willis returned to Pastor Rick's office. After she explained that every doorstep in town now had a feather on it, Pastor Rick simply said, "Good, now go back to every house and retrieve the feather from each doorstep."

"What!" Ms. Willis protested, "There's no way! By now those feathers will be scattered all over town!"

Pastor Rick, with just a hint of a smirk on his face responded, "Yes, Ms. Willis, that's precisely the point! And just like all those feathers, your words about Chuck and Mary can never be retrieved; by now they're scattered all over town!"

✝

So people, here's the moral of our story: if we aren't either part of the problem or part of the solution, let's please keep our pie-holes shut. And yes, I mean that in a loving, Christian sort of way. So the next time we are tempted to join in a nice juicy character assassination, let's just remember the *feather* sermon. Maybe that will remind us that once a malicious or untrue word leaves our lips, it can never be retrieved.

"Houston, we may have solved the problem."

But wait, there's more! Just when we all thought I was through fussing about gossip, I have another more subtle form of gossip we need to discuss. I call it *"prayer gossip."* The following is an example:

Joe calls Rick on Friday afternoon and during his casual conversation drops this bombshell: "I think the Feds may want to take over my bank...our liability to asset ratio is upside down." Fast-forward to Sunday morning.

It prayer time in Sunday school class and it is Rick's turn to pray. He prays his typical prayer and then slides in the big one: "Father God, please protect Joe's bank from financial ruin. You know he is very concerned about the feds taking it over and I pray you will give him the strength and wisdom to deal with this crisis." The news just revealed could add stature to Rick's reputation because his best friend is Joe, President and CEO of the largest bank in town. No one has this insider information but Rick. And he can't just go around repeating it in public because that would look like he is name-dropping or gossiping. Far be it from Rick to ever even as much as consider such a thing! But including it in a prayer, well, now that may be just his subtle way to let his classmates know that he is privy to some really inside scoop!

And yes, everybody is impressed. Well, everybody with the possible exception of God. I think he pretty much fails to see the humor in prayer gossip. Sorry Rick, but this kind of stuff might get us stuck in the *cheap seats* of heaven, and that's if we even make it at all!

Now don't get me wrong, I'm not saying we aren't supposed to pray for these kinds of situations. I'm just saying that leaking gossip or confidential information under the guise of prayer is a pretty suspect way of impressing people. If you really, really want to impress someone, I've got the perfect idea. Go out and buy about 50,000 copies of this book. I can assure you that I will be impressed! Now that's what I'm talking about!

Discussion Guide

1.   Just for grins, try to name the sermon topic that you have heard the most times during your life as a Christian:

_____

Now, try to name the sermon topic that you have heard the least:

_____

2.   In your opinion, what sermon topic do you feel needs to be preached more often?

_____

Why?

_____

Which sermon topic should be preached less?

_____

Why?

_____

3.   Have you heard a professing Christian gossip within the last month? _____ If so, what action did you, or should you have taken?

_____

If a Christian is caught in the act of gossiping, should they be called out on it? _____ Please explain how we might handle the situation:

_____

_____

_____

4.   On a scale of 1 to 10 with 10 being the most, how prevalent is gossip within the Christian community? _____ If

your answer was over a 5, do you feel we need more sermons on gossip? _____

5.   How might a non-believer react after hearing a Christian gossip?

_____

_____

6.   It has been said that gossip may be the sin most often committed by Christians. Do you agree? _____ If so, why do you think we gossip?

_____

_____

7.   Please name a scripture to share with your group that deals with gossip: _____
Please paraphrase the scripture:

_____

_____

_____

Notes:

Chapter Five

A Big Bunch of Chickens

I remember sitting in Sunday school class one morning when we were discussing evangelism. As usual, someone drew a line in the sand and we were all staking out our positions. It has always been my theory that once some of us Christians decide how we feel on a particular issue, we will try to justify it until the cows come home. On this particular morning the cows, in all their glory, were coming home.

Someone made the comment that far and away the best way to witness for Christ was to just live an exemplary life and other people would take notice. I agree that people will notice but I disagree with the notion that a person can live so stellar a life that folks will just flock to him or her begging and pleading to be told about Jesus. Isn't that just a touch on the prideful side? And Christians that are proponents of "the walk trumps the talk" scenario will sometimes quote St. Francis of Assisi, who said: "Preach the gospel at all times and when necessary, use words."

Here's the deal, some of us Christians are evidently afraid to go out and talk about Jesus Christ. It's probably because we fear that we might get rejected. I know I had that problem. So, in lieu of actually speaking with our mouth about God, we prefer to let our actions do the talking…and we will defend that position until the—you know what comes home. Another favorite quote is, "We can talk the talk but can we walk the walk?" Very catchy, but many of us Christians can walk the walk, but we are a little on the "scaredy-cat" side when it comes to talking the talk.

Now let's see what Jesus had to say on the subject. I make my point by using just one tiny little 3-letter word. Hint: It spells out a color. It's called *red*. Some of us may have noticed that Jesus filled up the gospels with *red*. Hello! Yes, those were HIS words! So maybe the next time we get the opportunity to witness to someone, we shouldn't just expose them to our exemplary life and then expect them to immediately want to jump on the Jesus band wagon. It takes *both*…a good walk and a good talk.

The story goes that a mid-western pastor made a proposal to both of his congregations one Sunday. He was a traveling minister and had two churches that were about twenty-five miles apart. When addressing his first congregation, he offered a fifty-dollar bill to anyone who would go down to the local Wal-Mart after church and "witness" to at least one person that the tooth fairy was real. Wait a minute! That must have been a typo…did I type the word "*tooth fairy*?" Yes I did, it's not a typo.

Later that morning during the sermon at his second church, he made a similar proposal. But instead of the tooth fairy, this time he requested that any volunteers should go to their Wal-Mart and "witness" to a least one person that *Jesus Christ* was real. And as with the first congregation, anyone that took him up on his offer would receive a fifty-dollar bill. The very next Sunday he preached a sermon on Christian courage, or the lack thereof. The meat of his sermon came from the previous week's challenge. A summary of that sermon is as follows:

"Last week I asked two different congregations to volunteer for two slightly different tasks. Each member of the first congregation received fifty-dollars if they would go down to Wal-Mart and witness to at least one person that the tooth fairly is real. I had thirteen takers. Then I traveled to the church of congregation number two and made a slightly different proposal.

There the volunteers received a fifty-dollar bill if they would visit their Wal-Mart and witness to at least one person that Jesus Christ is real. I only had two takers."

"So here we are, in a Christian church, a church that believes the word of God to be true and that we should follow those words. And several of those words in Matthew, chapter twenty-eight of the Holy Bible instruct us to go out and make disciples of men throughout the world. But it appears that a majority of us would rather sign folks up for the Tooth Fairy plan. Why? Simply put—I think the answer is *rejection*. Our little experiment proves one thing for sure. It's not that we are afraid to go out and talk to strangers; it's just that we are afraid to go out and talk to them about Christ. It seems like some of us Christians would almost rather someone die without salvation rather than having to face the two minutes of embarrassment and rejection we might experience while witnessing. People, I just don't think that is acceptable in God's eyes. He created us to be disciples, not a big bunch of chickens!"

Speaking of rejection let me tell a personal true story. It was October of 2002, and God had recently given me a business idea called the *Cross Reference*. It is a business directory, sort of like the *Yellow Pages* but featuring only Christians in business. It was my first actual day of going out and getting input from businessmen and women about the idea. I had just left my fifth appointment of the day and I was devastated. That fifth person had totally blown me out of the water, great idea and all. I had been rejected big time!

I will never forget exactly where I was, turning off Stanford Road onto Rosemont Drive in Panama City, Florida, when God sort of conked me over the head and said something to the effect of: "Bobby, are you kidding me? You have just spent the day talking to five Christians about your new business concept and four out of five think it's a fabulous idea! That is an amazing eighty percent! And now you are feeling rejected? Let me get this straight, you have a fairly decent plan and eighty percent of the people are accepting it? I on the other hand, have the PERFECT PLAN and eighty percent of the people are REJECTING IT!" Wow! I felt so ashamed of myself! From that day forward, my fear of rejection was no longer an option.

And finally, I want to close this chapter by telling about the best example of over-the-top courage I have ever heard. It's a little off topic but it is an outstanding example of courage. It goes like this:

A college professor was explaining to his class that for their final exam they must write an essay defining *courage*. Not just courage, but incredible courage! They could take as much time as they liked and could write as much as they wanted. After several questions from the students, the professor left the room and the test began. Approximately fifteen seconds later one young female student got up, handed her paper to the assistant and exited the room. Later that afternoon, the same student received an email from the professor. It simply read: "Your essay paper provided the greatest example of incredible courage I have ever seen. Your effort merits the highest grade I have awarded in my 36-year university career. Congratulations on your A-plus!"

Other than the student's name, date and class number, there were only two words written on her essay paper. Can you guess what those two words might have been? Give up? The two words she wrote to define incredible courage were simply, *"This is."* Think about it.

Do we have that kind of courage? There was no doubt this young lady had it. As they say in poker, she was "all in." For her there was no middle ground. She would either hit it out of the park or ground out to second. And knock it out of the park she did…we're talking a grand slam!

So please, for Christ's sake, let's not be a big bunch of chickens! We should have the kind of "risk it all" courage it takes to get out there and talk the talk! Sure, we might get rejected now and again…but hey, it's not like they're going to nail us to a cross.

Discussion Guide

1.   There are two trains of thought when it comes to the most effective way to evangelize. One is witnessing through your actions, the other is witnessing with your words. Which method do you prefer and why?

_____

_____

_____

2.   Have you ever had reservations about witnessing to someone? _____ Please explain:

_____

_____

_____

3.   Do you agree that the "fear of rejection" is more than likely the primary reason that we shy away from witnessing as often as we should? _____ If so, how might we best overcome this fear?

_____

_____

_____

4.   Have you ever been intimidated by a certain type of person when it comes to witnessing, yet have no problem whatsoever when it comes to another type of person? For instance, would it be easier for you to witness to a homeless person as opposed to a wealthy bank president or sports star? If so, why do you think that is?

_____

_____

_____

What do you think Jesus would say about your answer to the above question?

_____

5.   Name one or more scriptures that might help us with our fear of rejection when it comes to witnessing:

6.   If you would like, please share the circumstances surrounding the last time you witnessed to someone:

Notes:

Chapter Six

II Fred 3:16

Have you ever known a person that was exceptionally fun and intriguing to be around? Chances are when talking, the person in question had little if any clue what was about to come out of his or her mouth. And that's because each time they spoke, they did not set themselves up to be something they're not. For some of us, that's not the most prevalent of our Christian attributes, I'm afraid. A few of us Christians must have studied *Second Fred 3:16* where it evidently says something to the effect of: "Thou must trick the secular world into believing that we are something we're not." I have yet to find that verse in the Bible, but according to the way some of us act, it must be in there.

I once had an employee that was exceedingly fun and intriguing to be around. Janie was always the first one invited to a party, a luncheon, or for that matter, probably even one of those "parties" where they sell plastic pots. Hello! Anyway, the words *incredibly refreshing* come to mind when I think of her. I haven't seen Janie in over nineteen years and have no idea if she ever became a Christian. But I do know this—we need people like her on our side. When I think about Janie being a Christian and going out witnessing, it brings to mind someone showing up at a knife fight with an AK-47. In other words, she might not always win us over to her way of thinking but she would never fail to capture our attention.

When Janie got dressed in the morning, she didn't put on a mask. What we saw and what we heard is what we got, nothing more and nothing less. Janie was completely content with the way God made her and she didn't offer to lend him a helping hand. Well, that's not entirely true, she did slap five or six coats of paint on her face each morning, and for that, the world should be eternally grateful!

I wonder what it would be like to witness without a mask. I wonder what Janie would say when witnessing. I can only imagine the person being witnessed to and what their response would be to some of her comments. Maybe something like: "You did what? You ate lunch at Hooters? You bet on last night's football game? No way! And you got two speeding tickets last month? Are you kidding me?" Then we might just hear that person say something like this: "Hey, you're just like me. I thought all Christians were just perfect little angels; at least a lot of them act that way. But you're not like that at all."

And unless it was a typo, I think I once read in the Bible where we are supposed to confess our sins. So why not confess them while witnessing to a non-believer? Imagine the immense amount of credibility we Christians would gain if we just took off our masks and admitted to others that we aren't perfect?

Now, I've got an exercise we can try. First, let's pick out one of our favorite sins. It's okay if it's one of our white sins. White sins, by the way, are the big brothers of white lies. Someone once told me that white sins don't count off as much as full-blown, industrial strength sins. I think they read that in Second Revelation. Anyway, so far, so good...now let's try to practice confessing our sins in front of a mirror. I prefer bathroom mirrors over those church confessionals. Why? Because in our bathroom we will never hear a noise that sounds like the slapping of a knee, a loud snickering and then someone yelling: "Get outta here, you did not!"

Well, the big moment has finally arrived. It is time to take our new, unmasked self out into the real world and spread the word about Jesus, the Christ. I have found that one of the best ways to start a conversation with a non-believer is to ask them this simple question: "What's your opinion concerning the church?" Prepare for an ear-full, and ten to one says it won't be pretty. But at least we have them talking. Let's remember the point of this chapter; we need to witness completely *unmasked*. And during the conversation, always be on the lookout for an opportunity to let the person know that we also have our faults, our doubts, our fears, our skepticism or whatever.

I recall recently witnessing to a young man who had a whole laundry list concerning the "rules of religion" as he put it. He was telling me that Christianity just had too many rules, too many "dos," too many "don'ts." He admitted that he occasionally drank alcohol. I responded by telling him, "I had a beer last night." Folks, I wish I had had a camera. You cannot imagine the look of shock, disbelief and then RELIEF that came over his face. His whole demeanor changed. It was as if he had hit the *religion-lottery*!

Yes, thanks in part to the "holier-than-thou" lifestyle that some of us Christians portray to the secular world, he assumed that by drinking a beer he was headed straight to hell. And yes, for Christians out there that are cringing right about now, we did get into the discussion about abusing alcohol. We also talked about the fact that God may ultimately help him lose his desire to drink, especially if it ever began to affect his life. Folks, I'm not promoting alcohol, far from it; I'm just saying that the courage to take off our masks and admit our faults, whether sins or not, will gain us an immense amount of credibility as we witness to the secular world. By the way, I'm about ninety-three percent sure that the book of *II Fred* and the title of this chapter was the figment of someone's imagination…possibly mine.

Discussion Guide

1.   Why is it that some Christians (not you and me but all those other people) pretend to be someone they're not?

_____

_____

_____

For instance, sometimes we put on a "happy face" in spite of the fact that we are hurting inside. Is that healthy? _____ Why or why not?

_____

_____

_____

Are there other alternatives? _____ If yes, please give an example:

_____

_____

_____

2.   If we are feeling well and someone asks, "How are you doing today?" should we supply them with the details or just say, "Fine" and let it go at that?

_____

_____

Is it a lie to tell someone we are "_fine_" when we're not? _____
What is perhaps better response?

_____

_____

_____

3.   Do you know someone that rarely, if ever, puts up a front? _____ If yes, do you consider that refreshing? _____
Please elaborate:

_____

_____

4.   Where in the Bible does it say we should confess our sins to one another? _____

Would you like to confess a sin to your class or group? _____ If so, here's your chance:

5.   Do you agree with the notion that confessing a sin or fault while witnessing to a non-believer may gain us credibility? _____ Why or why not?

6.   Case Study: You are witnessing to a young woman about Christ and it comes up that she occasionally smokes pot. You have smoked pot twice in your life. Last month was one of those times. Do you tell her? _____ Why or why not?

Notes:

Chapter

Seven

The Nine-Second Rule

What is your favorite sin…gossiping, lusting, cheating, or a combination thereof? Personally, mine is *judging others*. Now don't get me wrong, I don't want a useful and oh-so-handy sin like *gossip* to get her feelings hurt. She surely deserves Top Ten status on my all-time favorite sins list. What would I do if I didn't have the sin of gossip to rely on when Hilda Jones wears that hideous green hat and outfit to church on Easter Sunday? I mean, seriously, doesn't Ms. Fashion Disaster realize that Easter is a *"pink"* day? I can't wait to tell my friends about Hilda's latest fashion train wreck!

But do we think that judging others is even more satisfying than gossip? I sure do! It tends to give me, as the judge, a power…a power not unlike that of God. Now, the Bible clearly states that if we're not God, judging others, especially in a demeaning and hypocritical way, is wrong. No problem, we can easily get ourselves off the hook. Right before we start the judging process, throw in some wonderful attributes of the person we are about to judge. Just remember to add the word *"but."* I had a friend explain to me that when someone says the word "but," you can always dismiss everything they said right before that word. "Ms. Jones is a wonderful housekeeper, but…" (Sorry, Mrs. Jones, evidently you're a terrible housekeeper).

I recall one Sunday evening when I wasn't judging, but…a fellow church member, Troy, stood up in the sanctuary and took credit for something he had very little to do with. He wasn't even sure of the name of the person that "he" had supposedly led to the Lord. Her name was Samantha but he called her Avis. In fact, I'm not so sure he had even met the person that had accepted Jesus earlier in the day. I had been working with Samantha for over a year. She was my trophy, not his. In my mind there was no way Troy could be a Christian; we don't do stuff like that. By the way, we don't call a new Christian a "trophy" either, but at the time I didn't have a clue.

Anyway, it sounds like this boy needed some industrial strength judging, huh? Well, believe me, when we got home from church that evening I appointed myself the *judge* and the *jury*. The entire court proceeding lasted no more than nine seconds—nothing like a little character assassination to finish up a wonderful day at church. And of course, when the accused doesn't show up to present a defense, well, we all know the results…*guilty as charged!*

Later that evening, I got this *Bobby; you inhale very rapidly* feeling inside. It was a feeling that seemed to be crying out to me, "Hey, dummy, you're even less of a Christian than the person you are accusing of not being a Christian!" Then it dawned on me…all the pleasure and satisfaction that God must have experienced when He used me to help lead Samantha to the Lord was wiped out by those few seconds of self-appreciating hogwash. But was that realization profound? Was it a turning point in my life? Of course not! I immediately forgot about the entire episode and continued merrily on my self-deceived, one-way journey to hell.

A few months later, I was at it again. I was in charge of the van ministry at our church and was going to be out of town for the weekend. By the way, weekends away, as I always referred to them, are when we get to skip church (not to mention tithing) and nobody knows the difference...with the possible exception of God. And then I just say, "Dear God, I would really love to be in our sanctuary this Sunday but I can worship in the bleachers while watching the Daytona 500 just as easily as I can in church." It's a great excuse, works well at Brave's games, too. Anyway, where was I?

Oh yeah, we had other volunteers for our van ministry. My job, if I wasn't driving, was to call and remind them when it was *their* turn to drive. We went to a retirement center and a low-income housing project to pick up folks for church. On this particular weekend, I needed someone to fill in for me since I would be "worshipping" in Daytona. I made my calls, but none were returned. But wait, I drove the van almost every other Sunday; the other drivers weren't called on but about once every other month. What's the deal? Didn't they realize I needed a break, too? Sounds to me like somebody needed a little judging, and far be it from me to pass up such an opportunity. "Ladies and gentlemen, start your judging!" And start I did.

But occasionally, just like any other hobby, judging has its problems. In this particular instance, the victim of my judging happened to be one of my friends. His name was Joe, a world-class individual. But hey, judging, just like progress, must go on. So naturally, I nailed poor Joe, not to the cross, but that's only because I didn't happen to have one at the time. Yes, I had called him early that morning and he had not returned my call. It was too late to get anyone else. I thought to myself of all the reasons he was probably going to hell. The poor guy was *toast*!

Then, several minutes after I had finished questioning and condemning Joe's entire existence, a funny thing happened. The phone rang...it was Joe, "Sorry I'm just getting back to you; we were on the boat all day. I'll be glad to drive tomorrow." I hate it when that happens! I felt like such a jerk, I should have known he would call. But those few seconds of judging sure felt good. It was almost like I wished he hadn't called. Then I could have a little more time to play God: the judge, the jury and the executioner.

But the story doesn't end there. God wasn't finished teaching me a lesson. I was pulling my suitcase out of the trunk when it hit me. Lucky for me, it wasn't a lightning bolt. No, it was just a thought. Actually, it was a book chapter, this book chapter, "The Nine-Second Rule." God had laid it on my heart that if I would just take the nine seconds it takes to judge someone and instead, use that time to pray for the person, two things would be accomplished.

First, I would spend that time doing something *constructive* instead of *destructive*. Maybe the person that I was going to judge needed prayer for the so-called indiscretion committed against me, or more than likely, for some other reason. Regardless, a nine second prayer beats a lifetime of satisfaction we could ever get from judging someone.

Secondly, I think about the massive waste of time I have spent doing good things for the Lord only to have them negated by my few seconds of judging. I have spent countless hours, maybe as many as several hundred working with our van ministry. In my opinion, now all those smiles that God got out of my efforts went down the drain the night I judged Joe.

And if that's not enough, remember the guy that "stole" my trophy? It turned out to be a simple mistake. He wasn't taking credit for something I had done; it was a simple case of mistaken identity. The bottom line…Troy and Joe certainly had grounds for a mistrial. Better yet, case dismissed!

Discussion Guide

1.   Unless you are Jesus, you sin. If you had to name the sin that you commit the most, what would it be? You may keep the answer to yourself or if you want to throw it out there for your group to discuss, go for it:

_____

_____

2.   It has been suggested that "judging others" is one of the most committed sins. Would you agree? _____ Why or why not?

_____

_____

_____

3.   Why do you think judging others is such a predominant sin?

_____

_____

_____

4.   Just for argument's sake, other than taking another person's life, what do you think is the least committed sin?

_____

Why?

_____

_____

5.   Case Study: John and Nancy recently became engaged and are now living together. Both are professing Christians. A mutual friend asks your opinion concerning the fact that they are living together. If you offer your opinion that you think their living together is wrong, are you being judgmental? _____ Why or why not?

_____

_____

_____

What if they are in fact living together, but not sleeping together...does that change the scenario? _____ Why or why not?

_____

_____

_____

6.   Is there a scripture in the Bible that permits judging under a specific set of circumstances? _____ If so, where is it found?

_____

_____

What is your interpretation of the scripture?

_____

_____

_____

Hint: 1 Cor. 2:15

Notes:

Chapter

Eight

Blue Collar Christians
& "The Question"

Have you ever noticed that we Christians, in general, are a touch prettier than the non-believers? Well, I personally tend to drag that percentage down, but most Christians are up in the 7, 8 or 9 range with an occasional 10 thrown in as a little icing on the church cake. And that, my friends, can be a problem. Why? Because some of us want to stay pretty; we don't want to get down and dirty. We don't want to venture into a smoky bar, a roach-infested apartment complex, or that creepy place the homeless guy sleeps to talk about Jesus. And that's the bad news.

The good news is that there is also a group of believers that I call B.C.'s or "blue collar" Christians. If you're reading this book, chances are that you fall into this category. I don't know if you're pretty or not, but I do know that blue collars don't mind getting their hands dirty for Jesus. When I say: "...if it weren't for us Christians, there'd be a lot more Christians," I'm not talking about the B.C.'s. The purpose of this chapter is to tell about a discovery I made that some of the blue collars out there might appreciate. So pour yourself a glass of sweet iced tea (blue collar Christians don't drink that unsweetened stuff and they certainly don't eat quiche), kick off your shoes, sit back and enjoy while I tell about "the question" that might knock your socks off, assuming you wear the silly things.

I recently attended an *Iron Sharpens Iron* conference at our church. It's a national men's ministry that teaches men how to act less like men…if you know what I mean. By the way, I highly recommend it. One of the seminars instructed us on leading people to Christ. The guy that taught it was evidently a world-class evangelist. He told us about a program that was designed to meet and witness to the "not as pretty as us" people. Actually, he didn't call it that, I did.

It all began by witnessing in a "not so pretty" neighborhood around his church—an area of mixed ethnicity and low income. Unfortunately, some Christians shy away from this type of evangelism because, well, it's just not neat and tidy. It is, for lack of a better word…*messy.*

He told us of a particular Wednesday night that a team (obviously a blue collar team) from his church began canvassing the "hood" in hopes of finding someone who would listen to their message. And here's the kicker…they had the most effective opening question for witnessing that I have ever heard. However, this is also the most *expensive* opening question anyone could ever use. Okay blue collars, hang on to your hats, here we go! The team would start the conversation by asking: "Do you have any unmet needs?

Were they nuts? Here they are in a low-income neighborhood asking an entire family if they have any unmet needs. And next I would suggest they ask if the pope is Catholic! Are you kidding me! No, they weren't kidding. So the father replies, "Well yes, as a matter of fact we do, none of our children have beds to sleep on." Un-cha-ching! There goes a quick five hundred dollars out the window. You'd get better odds in Vegas, for crying out loud!

Fortunately, it isn't about odds, it's about *souls.* And what better way to get someone's attention than to let them know we care. Remember the old saying: "People don't care how much we know until they know how much we care." Asking a person or family if they have any unmet needs just screams: "I care about you, I really do!"

Later that night, the team met back at the church and one member summed it up like this: "If the children in that family wake up tomorrow morning without beds, we're bogus." So the question became…would the witnessing team put their money where their mouth is? Has anyone priced a new bed lately? They are a little less than the price of a new Kia, but not much. But let it suffice to say that the very next morning three young kids in the hood woke up in brand new beds. Instant credibility established…big time!

We weren't told the rest of the story but we can be sure of one thing, the next time members of that church come around, I'm betting the family will be more than willing to listen to anything they have to say. And I have one last bet…and that is that if we have the courage to go to those "not so pretty places" and ask the question: "Do you have any unmet needs?" God will not only bless us, but He will make a way where there is no way. After all, if He can create a universe, I'm thinking He can come up with three new beds now and again! Good night, John Boy.

Discussion Guide

1.   After reading Chapter 8, in your own words please define a "blue collar" Christian:

_____

_____

Do you consider yourself a blue collar Christian? _____
Please elaborate:

_____

_____

2.   You may have heard that in the typical church, twenty percent of the people do eighty percent of the work. Do you

agree? _____ If so, would you define the twenty percent as blue collar Christians? _____ Why do you think the percentage is so low?

_____

_____

_____

What could be done to increase the percentage of blue collar Christians?

_____

_____

_____

3.   In this chapter it was stated that asking someone if they have any "unmet needs" is a good way (in certain situations) to start off a witnessing conversation. Do you agree? _____
Why or why not?

_____

_____

_____

What other questions would you suggest that might open the door to a successful witnessing conversation?

_____

_____

_____

4.   What, in your opinion, are the main mistakes we as Christians make when sharing Christ with others?

_____

_____

_____

5.   If you have one, please share with the group your favorite "witnessing" story.

Chapter

Nine

Pulling the Wings
Off of Butterflies

Not all schools of theology are created equal. And evidently, not all professors of theology are created equal either. For those of us who have known a seminary student, we may have heard a comment similar to this: "Wow! I just finished ABC School of Christian Theology and believe it or not, I still believe in Jesus!"

It sounds like I'm making that up, huh? Sorry folks, I'm not. I hesitate to say this but word on the street is that the above comment is not as rare as we might imagine. Yes, I'm afraid some of our seminary professors may take liberties with God's word that would make Noah get back on the boat. Now I don't know about you, but that sounds pretty un-American to me. I bet some of these professors are so un-American that they don't even drive Japanese cars. How un-American is that!

Here's a supposedly true story told to me by a friend who attended a major seminary college in the Southeast. He started by telling me that if students don't have a pretty strong faith before they get to seminary, they are *toast* by the time they get out. He had a classmate that evidently couldn't take it anymore. One day at the beginning of an Old Testament seminar, his classmate actually stood up and made the following rather sarcastic announcement: *"About two weeks after I got here, I was told the Easter Bunny was just a figment of someone's imagination. A week later my entire childhood experience was redefined when they told me there was no Santa Claus. Soon after that I had a professor shoot down the Tooth Fairy concept. And let's not forget my silly ideas about the Bible...I should have known that much of the Old Testament, as my professor repeatedly pointed out, was just folklore.*

Folklore, according to him, of biblical proportions...and speaking of biblical, we are not allowed to capitalize the word Bible in his class. Anyway, since my instructor has finished his task of dismantling and rebuilding my entire thought process, he doesn't have much to keep him busy. So now, he just passes time by sitting in front of the class pulling the wings off butterflies."

Hello! Maybe it was just a typo, but I could have sworn that I read in the Bible that if we don't have the faith of a little child, we will never get to play on the swing sets of heaven. Now don't get me wrong, I'm not saying that the seminary professors in question were ever children, but teaching that the Old Testament is largely folklore? C'mon! Sounds to me like those professors would be better off teaching evolution at *berkley.* Now there is a "b" word nobody in his or her right mind would ever capitalize.

However, my friends, there is some good news. For the time being at least, the seminary alluded to above has settled out of court and agreed to allow students to continue to put a capital "J" in front of the word *esus.* (No "j" in front of the word esus)

Let me conclude by saying that the vast majority of seminary schools and professors that teach in them are wonderful. It's just like with anything; one bad egg can give the whole carton a tarnished name. Here is an actual example: I sent this chapter to a friend who happens to be an ordained minister. Here is a quote from his response: "One guy in Ohio told me that when he got out of an extremely liberal seminary he wasn't sure what he believed anymore and so he met with his district superintendent to share that concern. His DS had the same experience and told him to do what he did... 'Take your Bible, go into the woods and get yourself straightened out.'"

This brings us to the bottom line:

A 4-year trip to a liberal seminary...$60,000.

A 4-day trip to the woods...*priceless!*

Discussion Guide

Due to the fact that Chapter 9 does not lend itself to producing suitable discussion topics, we are going to try something a little different this time. During the course of my 13 years of being a Christian, I have heard several questions that caused intense controversy among the people trying to answer them. I thought it might be interesting to ask some of those same questions and let your group join the fray. Please try to keep fistfights down to an absolute minimum. (Smiley face goes here).

1.   In a recent sermon, a pastor stated that he believed that Judas Iscariot went to heaven, as opposed to hell. What is your belief concerning Judas' eternal destination and why?

_____

_____

_____

2.   We know that God can "hear" any prayer, but does He concern himself with the prayers of the wicked? _____ Does John 9:31 settle this matter? _____ Why or why not?

_____

_____

_____

3.   Some Christians believe that "once saved, always saved" and some do not. What do you believe and why?

_____

_____

_____

_____

What scripture backs up your position?

_____

4.   What is your take on the "doctrine of election," which is also known as predestination?

_____

_____

5.   It has been said that there are probably more women in heaven than men because women are typically better at relationships i.e. a relationship with Christ. Do you give any credibility to that theory—why or why not?

_____

_____

_____

_____

Notes:

Chapter

Ten

That Ain't No Bull

Some of our readers may have heard the results of a recent study concerning the lies we tell on a daily basis. The study discovered that Americans tell an average of about *three lies* per hour, but only while we're awake. That is surprising to me because I know a few people that I'm positive could tell a lie in their sleep. In fact, I used to be one of them.

The study went on to say that lying was the "fabric" that held America together. I'm thinking that's a pretty sad commentary on our nation. Supposedly, according to this study, lies facilitate human interaction. "How do I look honey?" "You look great, darling!" Now there's a whopper! And I hate to admit it, but back before Jesus showed up in my life, I probably only told three *truths* per day…if that many.

Speaking of lying, I suppose now is the time to get it off my chest, to tell about my pathetic and distasteful background. Ah yes, the pre-Jesus days. I wrote the book on lying. Actually it was a newspaper. Seriously, you'll see what I mean in a minute; right now I'm just praying most of you will just skip this chapter and head straight to *eleven*. But for those few unlucky ones, well, here we go.

By 1990 I had opened hundreds of clothing stores throughout America and was living the life of luxury. The only thing missing in my life was Jesus. But what did I need him for? I was making a boatload of money each month and doing just fine. So, as he often does, God tried to get my attention by helping me fly the chain of almost 1,000 ladies' discount clothing stores into the side of a mountain.

Bankruptcy, here we come! Think that got my attention? Well, of course not! Just because I lost everything, including my family, why should that be a wake-up call? As far as I was concerned, the worst part was going from a new Mercedes to a rusted out '79 Caprice Classic, virtually overnight. I will admit that was just a touch on the embarrassing side.

And my biggest worry...how in the world was I going to be able to afford my scotch? I think the devil heard my concern and decided to help me with my next business venture, starting a newspaper called *Beach Bull*. As I mentioned before, it was a disgusting little rag that featured dirty jokes, half-naked women and of course, a ton of lies. My greatest ambition was to scam my readers, all twelve of them, into believing what I printed. And believe me, they did! Would any of y'all like me to tell about two of my biggest coups? I was afraid of that. Okay, here goes nothing:

Now keep in mind, we were printing 50,000 copies of the newspaper every month. In about June of 1991, the headline of *Beach Bull* read: "**LOCAL BEACHES TO CLOSE FOR 3 MONTHS.**" The story said something to the effect of: "...because the beautiful white sands of Panama City Beach had become a bit on the dingy side, the TDC (Tourist Development Council) had hired the Clorox Bleach Company to come and bleach our sands back to a nice, bright white color."

I thought that was pretty funny. The TDC did not. It seems that a few days after the "bleach the beach issue" hit the newsstands, the phones lit up from one end of the beach to the other. People from Alabama and Georgia were calling to cancel their hotel reservations. I never knew people from those two states were so gullible. Oh wait, I graduated from elementary school in Georgia and high school in Alabama. Never mind. Anyway, needless to say, the beach hotel and motel owners failed to see the humor in my little scam. I never did find out how many cancellations they actually ended up with, but one beach businessman used the words *financial carnage* to describe it.

But our biggest coup was the "free gas coupon" issue of *Beach Bull*. We put a coupon in the paper that offered ten dollars worth of free gas at all participating Jr. Stores, a local convenience store chain in the Panama City area. There was only one slight catch...there were NO participating stores.

About twenty-four hours after that issue of the *Bull* came out, my phone rang. It was Mr. Scott Coffman, the director of marketing for the Jr. Stores. He politely screamed into the phone, "Bobby, are you crazy?" Naturally, I played dumb and asked what he was so upset about. He told me that hundreds of people were trying to use the coupons with surprising amounts of success. I countered that the coupon disclaimer clearly said: "at participating stores only." That's when he explained in no uncertain terms that his customers were not necessarily the sharpest knives in the drawer. They would pump the gas first (back in the early 90's we could still do that) and then march into the store with nothing but a coupon and not a dime to their name, just the coupon. For some strange reason, the relationship between *Beach Bull* and the Jr. Stores started to deteriorate after that.

So as you can imagine from the above stories, I know a few things about lying, which brings me to the point of the chapter. Some of us, whether intended or not, tell lies. Or at least, we say things that don't necessarily come to pass. I'm not referring to the mean spirited, intentional lies. I'm referring to stuff that comes out of our mouth that just isn't necessarily true. I looked up *lie* in the dictionary. Some of the definitions were: untruth, fib, falsehood, deceit and dishonesty.

So for instance, what about when I tell John I will call him tomorrow about the fifty dollars I owe him and he never hears from me? Is that a lie? I don't know if most of us would call it a lie, but I think we can all agree at the very least it is a *falsehood*. I said I would do something and I did not do it. So what does all this have to do with us Christians? Well, I believe for some of us Christians, this kind of behavior is just SOP (standard operating procedure). We say we will do something one minute and the next minute any thought about following up on what we just said is history. We, of all people, should mean what we say, and say what we mean.

As an experiment, I kept up with these little indiscretions for a day. How many times would a professed Christian do less than what he or she said they would in a twenty-four hour period? All of these incidents involved professing Christians.

Here we go:

Incident 1: Sam told me he would be at my house between 9:00 and 9:30 a.m. on Tuesday morning to discuss a business matter. He did not show up and he didn't call.

Incident 2: Susie told me she would call me later in the afternoon to give me a decision on the Dothan, Alabama, territory where she wanted to start a publication. I had met with her four times to help her in starting a business with no upfront investment. I had gone out of my way to help her. She never even had the courtesy to call and say, never mind.

Incident 3: I told a friend I would pray for his surgery. I must admit that the thought never crossed my mind again until I heard that the operation was over and he was doing just fine. Yes, my friends, I am as guilty as anyone of saying one thing and doing another.

Incident 4: Carl owed me almost $400. The payment was about sixty days past due and I called to find out when I could expect payment. Carl's response was: "I thought we had already paid that." His comment came after he had received several invoices in the mail. But I gave him the benefit of the doubt; maybe he really did think he had paid it. He indicated he would take care of it...but a week later, still nothing. I sent him one last invoice, and after not receiving payment, I called again. I am never pushy when collecting money because the good Lord knows I have been late on payments before. I don't even put the words "past due" on a late invoice...it just seems a little harsh. But this time Carl was rude. His snappy response was, "I said I would take care of it!" As of this writing, he never has.

✝

The above incidents all happened in one day. And as I said, these people are professing Christians. Now we all have bad days and we certainly aren't perfect, but we tend to forget that the many in the secular world has us under a microscope. Think about it this way: if our word doesn't mean anything when dealing with our brothers and sisters in Christ, just imagine how we will deal with someone from the secular world. And some of them are just waiting to discover one more way they can justify dismissing Christianity. Let's not give it to them.

So the next time we say that we are going to call someone, or that we will pay someone, or that we will pray for someone, then as that Nike commercial says: "Just do it!"

But just as important is this—let's all have the courage that when we can't call, or when we can't pay, or when we don't pray, or when we don't do something that we said we were going to do, let's just step up to the plate and admit it. That's the kind of "right stuff" that makes God smile...and that ain't no bull!

Discussion Guide

1.   Most would agree that murder is the least committed sin. But do you also agree that lying is more than likely the one of the most committed sins? _____ If you agree, why do you think that is?

_____

_____

_____

2.   What is your definition of a "white lie?"

_____

_____

Do you think God differentiates between "white lies" and those real "whoppers? _____
Why or why not?

_____

_____

3.   Case Study: You are having coffee with a non-believer at a McDonalds in Wal-Mart. He has lots of questions about Jesus and is showing signs of coming to Christ. He is a homeless man who is obviously down on his luck and even showing signs of malnutrition. One day during your typical Tuesday afternoon visit, he excuses himself to go to the restroom. As he is returning, you notice him open a pack of bread from the bakery and slip several buns into his pocket. He returns to your table and you continue the conversation. A manager approaches your table and asks your friend if he took some bread from the bakery. He denies it. The manager then asks you if you have any knowledge of the situation. What do you do? If you tell the manager you saw your friend steal the bread, you risk alienating him and any future discussions about Christ. On the other hand, is your only other alternative to lie? Please share with the group your analysis of the situation.

_____

_____

_____

_____

4.   A main theme of Chapter 10 is that some of us Christians promise things and then fail to ever give it another thought. In other words, what we promise never happens. How might a non-believer assess our lack of follow through?

_____

_____

_____

_____

_____

Notes:

Chapter Eleven

Building a Better Grease Factory

Please raise your hand if are a member of a Christian small group. Does your group have a monthly project to help the elderly? Does your group have a monetary fund set up in case someone needs financial assistance? Does your group occasionally go to one of the small group members' house to have a "fix it up" day? Does your group ever go into a low-income area to see if any of the residents have unmet needs that your group might possibly help with? Does your group seek out people that need an occasional ride to the grocery store, a beauty parlor or a doctor's appointment?

If your group would have to answer "no" to most or all of the above questions, I just have one question…wouldn't you like to see your group have more of an impact on the community? I used to be in a small group that didn't get out into the community very often. It was comprised of primarily new, and a few of us "rough around the edges" Christians. I called the group Moon Finger. That's because at one time or another, both names, shall we say, got *shot*. But that's another story. By the way, I have always wanted to thank Scott Tolbert publicly for hosting the group for almost four years in his home. Thanks, Scotty! You get 750 points.

Anyway, each week we met, we fellowshipped, we worshiped, we ate some pretty serious vittles and then we went home. Oh yes, we also talked a lot about going out into the community. But we hardly ever did it. However, I do remember one time when we actually got off our duffs and went into a housing project to pray with and for the residents. And do you know what? An elderly black gentleman accepted Christ while we were there. So why in the world didn't that encourage us to get out more? I don't know, but I take full responsibility for that mistake...it's something I'll always regret.

A lot of small groups out there might be compared to the world's greatest grease factory. In case any of our readers are not familiar with the grease factory syndrome, here's the scoop:

Once upon a time in the Land of Odd, there was a grease factory that grew and grew and became the largest, most famous grease factory in the entire world. Like all the other places in Odd, it was located exactly 17.3 miles from nowhere. Some referred to it as the Disney World of grease factories.

People flew in from all over the world to visit and tour this humongous manufacturing facility. And in lots of ways, it was just like Disney World. It was a sprawling two hundred acres that had amusements, restaurants and even the famous "Grease Monkey." Dressed in full costume (and a bit grease-stained, if you will) this iconic character walked around kissing babies, taking photographs with the kids and lubing squeaky rides. And of course, his nickname was Monkey Mouse (I couldn't resist that one).

Over the years the grease factory gradually added tour guides that would drive little miniature trains around showcasing the property to visitors. The tour guides would announce over their loud speakers interesting facts about the factory and its history. At the end of the tour, the guides would take a few questions from their tourist visitors. On this particular day, a visitor from England asked his tour guide, "Tell me please, where does this, the world's largest grease factory, sell all of the grease that it makes?" It was like the world came to a screeching halt! The crowd could have heard a pin drop. The tour guide was obviously stunned by the question. After regaining his composure, he answered rather indignantly: "Sell it? Are you kidding me, sir? I'll have you know it takes every ounce of the grease we manufacture just to keep this factory running!"

So there we have it, a large human endeavor that had absolutely no impact on its community or the world, whatsoever. Is your small group like the grease factory, very little, if any, impact on the community? If you answered "*yes*" that is a good thing. Why? Because this is the first and most important step in solving the problem.

I recall a few years back going through the *40 Days of Purpose* study by Rick Warren. One thing stood out to me from that study that I still remember to this day. Rick said, and I must paraphrase: "the last thing some of us need is another Bible study." What he was saying was that we need to get off of our *keister's* (my word, not his) and go out and put into practice what we have learned in all those studies. What good is studying the Bible if we don't venture out into the world and put its principals into practice? Seems like I read somewhere that faith without works is dead. Hmmm, where was it that I read that?

Anyway, I joined another small group called Characters for Christ. And I must take this opportunity to thank Gen-Rule Todd and Stacey "Highway Girl" Breitmann for hosting the Characters group (you guys get 1,500 points). Now, one of the first things we did was to read and study a book on small groups. The title of the book is *Why Small Groups?* by C.J. Mahaney. This book takes an in-depth look at the structure of a small group, its purpose, and even why a leader should be chosen. We read this book as if it were a weekly study, which took about two months. An outstanding book and I recommend it without reservation.

The book suggested the group have a purpose and accompanying mission statement. I, on the other hand, was perfectly fine with just meeting, fellowshipping, drinking coffee and going to the house. But fortunately, some of our group members took that "purpose thing" to heart. Evidently, they weren't interested in becoming another grease factory. So not surprisingly…soon after finishing the book, we scheduled our first "fix up day" for a co-member of the group.

I scrambled for excuses…my back hurts, my wife's back hurts, my entire neighborhood's backs hurt…my daughter married a Democrat…the Beatles might reunite…our birdbath needs emergency refinishing …it didn't matter, any excuse to get me out of ruining my Saturday morning. Fortunately, my small group didn't fall for any of my lame excuses.

And what a blessing our project turned out to be for all involved! We showed up at the target house about 8 a.m., and for the next several hours there were about nine or ten of us running around like a bunch of sprayed roaches. We were mowing, planting, cutting, chopping, laughing, sweating and telling an occasional whopper. Anyway, the only "grease" that we saw was coming from our elbows.

And finally, in the true spirit of Christian friendship, we had a collective incentive if we finished our project by noon… we could all share in an ice-cold keg. Yep, there's nothing better after a hard Saturday morning's work than to sit back, relax and sip a tall cool one from an ice-cold keg of…*milk,* reduced fat, no less.

Discussion Guide

1.   Does your church actively promote small groups within its membership? _____ If not, is it something you or your Sunday school class might promote? _____ If you agree small groups are an important part of a church, please elaborate:

_____

_____

2.   Are you a member of a small group or Sunday school class? _____ If so, what is the primary advantage of being a member?

_____

_____

3.   Rick Warren once said something to the effect of, *"the last thing some of us need is to be in another Bible study, it's time we get out and put into practice what we've learned."* Do you agree with that statement? _____ Why or why not?

_____

_____

_____

4.   Does your Sunday school class or small group have a mission statement? _____ If so, what is the primary purpose of the group?

_____

_____

_____

5.   Is your group actively involved in the community? _____ If not, is there something you could do as a group to impact your community? _____ If so, what might that be?

_____

_____

6.   If you were the leader of your small group or Sunday school class, what is the one thing you might suggest to increase the effectiveness of the group?

_____

_____

7.   Have you ever been involved in a "grease factory" type group? _____ If so, how would you describe the experience?

_____

Notes:

Chapter

Twelve

Complain About This

As Ms. Langston enters the department store, all *heaven* breaks loose! Graffiti starts falling from the ceiling, a ragtime band begins playing, horns are blowing and balloons fill the air. "Congratulations!" booms across the store's public address system: "You, my good lady, are our one millionth customer!" Ms. Langston has just hit the proverbial jackpot! The store manager presents her with a brand new washer & dryer, a new bedroom suite, other various prizes and a store credit card worth $5,000! The gala event continues for another fifteen minutes and ends with Ms. Langston cutting the ribbon to celebrate the opening of a brand new section of the store.

When the festivities are finally over, Ms. Langston thanks the store manager for the over twenty thousand dollars worth of cash and prizes she has won and continues to where she was headed in the first place…the *complaint department*.

Does this remind us of anybody? I know who it reminds me of…it reminds me of *me*! Here I am, one of the most blessed people living in the richest nation on earth, and I grumble and complain like a homeless beggar in Afghanistan. What's up with that? And what kind of signal does it send to the non-believer? I recently realized that if I was a non-believer and heard someone like me fussing and complaining all the time, I wouldn't want any part of Christianity either.

My wife used to be a complainer, too. We made a good team, we could out-complain just about anybody. One week I would out-complain her, the next week she would take me down. Vicki finally won the title, "Complainer of the Year," when the following event took place:

We were visiting our daughter in Asheville, North Carolina, one weekend and decided to attend her church. About ten minutes into the service, as they were passing the plate, my wife asked the usher if he would mind turning the air-conditioner down, for it was way too hot (I have no clue whether turning an air-conditioner *down* makes it hotter or colder, I just leave that up to the women folk). Anyway, he said he would be delighted to and all was well…for at least three to four more minutes.

Then she again motioned for him to come over to our pew where she asked him if he would mind turning the air-conditioner *up*, for it was getting way too cool. This happened five or six more times during the service…up, down, up, down. As we were leaving, I spotted the usher who was involved and thanked him for being so understanding about the constant badgering from my wife. He said, "Oh, no problem, it didn't bother me at all. We don't have an air-conditioner."

Okay, I admit it, that was a joke, but it wasn't really that much of a stretch from reality. Fortunately, we both finally realized that our attitudes could affect the way people looked at Christianity. What if we actually scared someone off from the faith because of our demeanor? What if the title of this book was: *If It Weren't For Bobby and Vicki, There'd be A Lot More Christians?* I'm trying to imagine what God would say? Seriously, we're standing in front of Jesus on judgment day and he might say something like: "So Bobby, I hear you were never happy with what I gave you. It seems you complained about this or you fussed about that. And do you know that some of your constant complaining actually drove folks away from me? Well, I've got an idea, why don't you go visit them in a place called…well, you know. By the way, although it really needs one, the place you're headed to is just like that church you were in…it doesn't have an air-conditioner either!"

Let's cut to the chase. Someone once told me: "In many cases when we complain about something, we're just telling God that he didn't do a good enough good job." Let's not go there, folks…if you know what I mean.

Discussion Guide

1.   What do you think Christians complain about the most. Take three guesses.

A.

_____

B.

_____

C.

_____

Raise your hand if you ranked *"finances/money"* as number one. You win a cookie! Yes, we Christians are no different than anyone else when it comes to complaining. But the fact is, if you are a typical American with a house, a car and a household income of over $35,000 a year—you rank in the top two percent of the world's richest people. Why do you think we continue to complain if that statistic is accurate?

_____

_____

_____

2.   How might our complaining affect a non-believer's view of Christianity?

_____

_____

_____

3.   Do you know a Christian that is a chronic complainer? _____ If yes, without naming names, describe the person's behavior:

_____

_____

_____

Why do you think they complain?

_____

_____

_____

Do you think they realize that they complain so much? _____ If not, is there perhaps a gentle way you could discuss the matter with them? _____ Ask your group for suggestions. List what you consider the best suggestions here:

_____

_____

_____

4.   Give an example of the last time you complained and if in hindsight, it was justified:

_____

_____

_____

5.   Please name a scripture that deals with complaining:

_____

_____

_____

Chapter Thirteen

"Bible Boat Bull"

Here's a biggie! Objections to the Christian faith are wonderful! What? Yes, I said wonderful. When a person has an objection, any objection to the Christian faith, we've got them talking. And most people don't talk just for the sake of talking…well, if we leave my sister out of the equation. She can talk five hundred WPM (Words per Minute) with gusts up to six hundred. Anyway, when we hear an objection to our faith, it's time to shut up and listen.

I used to sell pre-owned cars. And believe it or not, I actually sold one. Yep, that's right, *one*. I was even nominated as the "Worst Used Car Salesman in America" by a leading publication. One of the reasons I was so bad was because I didn't listen, I yapped. I looked up "yapping" in the dictionary. It is defined as: *talking for no apparent reason.*

I was a yapper. A used car customer might say, "This eighty-nine Ford truck is too expensive and I bet it doesn't get good gas mileage." That should have meant to me that if the price was lower and it had reasonable fuel economy, he might bite. So naturally, I yapped. I would say something like, "Are you kidding me? We're losing over five hundred dollars just by selling this cream puff; and as far as the gas mileage is concerned, our mechanic just put a new fuel-saving device on it. As a matter of fact, I took it out for a spin yesterday, and after driving about four miles, the fuel tank overflowed!" How's that for answering his objection? Pretty pathetic, huh! Here this guy is, indicating he might be interested in a vehicle on my lot, and I treat his objections like a joke.

Unfortunately, that's how some of us treat the objections to Christianity. I once heard a story about a young man that had serious issues with Christianity because of what he referred to as "bible boat bull." He was alluding to the story in Genesis about Noah loading up about a zillion animals in the ark right before the forecast went south. This guy couldn't buy into something like that. It was just too preposterous! It sounded to him like a fairytale of biblical proportions. And guess what? When I first read Genesis, I had the same reaction. In fact, I even wrote a satirical story about it...see below:

✝

God: "Noah, build me an ark."
Noah: "Build you a what?"
God: "An ark, you know...a boat."
Noah's Wife: "What did he say?"
Noah: "Build him an ark."
Noah's Wife: "Build him a what?"
Noah: "That's what I said."
God: "You better get cranking, it's gonna rain for forty days and forty nights."
Noah's Wife: "What's he talking about?"
Noah: "He thinks we're in Seattle."
God: "And you're gonna be swim-less in Seattle if you don't get to it!"
Noah: "Where do I get the materials?"
Noah's Wife: "Call Home Depot."
Noah: "I did. The recording said they won't be open for another few thousand years."
God: "And I want it filled with animals...a male and female of each species."

Noah: "You're not serious! Can you imagine a lion and a zebra on the same boat?"
God: "Good point! Take along some extra lion food."
Noah: "Okay, what do they eat?"
God: "Zebras, you dummy!"
Noah: "The wife has one request."
God: "What is it, Noah?"
Noah: "She wants to know if we can take along the necessities."
God: "Like food and water?"
Noah: "No, like Glade and cat litter."
God: "Good point, now get to work before I get angry!"
Noah: "Get angry and do what, for instance?"
God: "Get angry and revise the forecast, for instance!"
Noah: "Good point! Going to work here, Boss!"

†

Fortunately for me, I had a very understanding mentor (hello Randy McInvale) that took each of my questions and objections and treated them as if they were the most legitimate issues and concerns in the world. Sadly, some of us Christians don't handle objections that way. If I've heard it once, I've heard it a number of times: "That person is just looking for an excuse, any excuse, to get out of going to church." And that just may be true...but what if it's not? Would we want to blow off a person's objection only to find out later that they were indeed seeking to learn more about Christianity? How would we feel to stand in front of Jesus and justify that one? No thanks, brother, not for me!

Back to the "bible boat bull" objection...what should we say to a person who raised such an issue? In my opinion, the first thing we should do is to acknowledge the objection as being valid. Then, if we have ever had similar concerns, share them with the person: "Yes, I can relate to that. When I first read that in the Bible I thought that Noah and the ark story was bogus, too." With that simple gesture, we have gained two things, their attention and their respect. The fact that we, as "signed up and practicing Christians" have also had those issues will help us gain the credibility we need to further the conversation. Even if their objection is the most ridiculous thing we have ever heard, we should treat it as legitimate.

So I've been thinking how I, as author of this book, would respond to a person who said: "I just can't get past the ark story in Genesis?" After agreeing with him that I had similar misgivings, I believe I would say something like this: "What about a tiny cell, much less in size than that of a pinhead, which grows into a full size human being? Or how about the atmosphere of the earth...if our planet was either several miles closer or farther from the sun, we would either burn up or freeze to death? Was it pure coincidence that earth ended up the precise distance from the sun to give us the perfect atmosphere to sustain life? When I think about it, those things are almost as amazing to me as Noah and the ark. But we're all different and I think God may use various methods and miracles to speak to each one of us individually."

I might continue the conversation as follows: "Just like Noah and the ark are to you, my biggest objection when I first started considering Christianity was planet earth. The theory of evolution suggests the world is millions and millions of years old, yet most Christians seem to believe otherwise. But if the world isn't millions of years old, why for instance, does it have all those strata of different colors of sand and gravel in the Grand Canyon, each representing a different pre-historic age? Someone shed some possible light on that phenomenon by asking me this simple question... 'In the very beginning of Genesis in the Bible, what were the approximate ages of Adam and Eve?' Well, I knew they weren't infants, because they covered themselves with fig leaves to hide their nakedness, and I suspected they weren't too old since they didn't yet have children. Therefore, my guess was that they were probably middle age."

My friend replied, "Precisely, and if God could make Adam and Eve begin their lives at middle age, he could also create planet earth to begin its existence at middle age. Hence, the physical evidence that makes the earth look older than it actually is might have been God's design." I'm not saying this is fact; I'm just saying it is as plausible as any of the other theories out there.

I'm not suggesting our readers necessarily respond this way, this is only an example of how I might respond. And it doesn't really matter what a person's objection is. The fact that they have an objection is the point. And speaking of objections, theirs just may be the starting point for another soul spending eternity with Jesus Christ. So let's listen to the objections, regardless of how frivolous, and then treat them like someone's life depends on it...because it does!

Discussion Guide

1.   In your opinion, what is the number one objection to the Christian faith from the secular world?

Why do you think that is the main objection?

---

2.   How would you respond if a non-believer said that he or she did not want any part of Christianity because of all the hypocrites in church?

---

3.   How would you respond if a non-believer said that he or she will go to heaven because they are just as "good of a person" as you?

---

4. How would you respond if a non-believer said that he or she did not believe because of all the "fairy tales" in the Old Testament?

_____

_____

5. Do you agree with the statement that although it may sound preposterous, any excuse or reason a non-believer uses to shun Christianity is legitimate…at least in their eyes? Some say that regardless of whether an excuse or reason is legitimate or not, if the non-believer uses it, we as Christians should treat it as legit. Do you agree? _____
Why or why not?

_____

_____

_____

6. Have you ever witnessed to a non-believer that voiced his or her objections? _____ If so, please share the objections and how you responded:

_____

_____

_____

7. Have you have had a witnessing experience "gone bad? If so, please explain:

_____

_____

_____

_____

Chapter Fourteen

All the Credibility of an Infomercial Host...

Let's use our imaginations for a moment. One day Satan was attempting to come up with the world's biggest scam to trick people into believing his lies. Naturally, he had tried sex, drugs and let's not forget rock and roll. In fact, he even brought out the big guns with wealth, power and popularity. People were falling for his lies by the thousands. Oh sure, all the sins were doing their jobs, but the devil wanted something better, something that would completely fool unsuspecting humans. He wanted something that would affect not thousands, but millions. He wanted something so powerful it might cancel out even the goodness of God. What could it be?

This was a tough chore so Satan decided to just take the afternoon off and ponder on it for a while. Besides, after he had helped jump-start sins a few thousand years ago, they seemed to be doing just fine on their own. So Satan prayed a little prayer to himself, rolled up a big ole fat doobie, poured a tall bourbon & water and settled down to watch the tube. "Wait!" He screamed, "What did I just do? Settle down to watch the what? The tube? That's it! The tube! I'll use television...it reaches millions. Ah ha, I've finally figured it out!" And what about the prayer he said to himself? Well, it was about to be answered...big-time!

"Just say *hell no* to hell!" the big-haired woman on TBM network was yelling. "And to help our viewers say *hell no* to hell, Brother Dave has a new CD out that you can buy for as little as fifty dollars down and twenty-five a month! But wait, there's more! Have your credit card ready, call within fifteen seconds, and we'll throw in two jiggers of forgiveness absolutely free! And... as a highly exclusive offer to the first ninety million that call, we have discounted shipping and handling down to a mere arm and a leg...while supplies last!"

Satan slapped his forehead and declared, "Why didn't I think of that before? What a wonderful way to scam the world. Since people are gullible anyway, all they need is a little legitimate convincing and I've got 'em! And what better way to legitimize something than to put it in print or on television. Wow! This is gonna be sweet!"

Now don't get me wrong readers, it wasn't quite the piece of cake that the devil thought it was going to be. First, he had that splinter in his side, Billy Graham, to deal with. And there were others, on-air preachers like Max Lucado, Rick Warren and Charles Stanley that actually believe what they preach. But if Satan could get enough bogus TV evangelists on the air, it would diminish the reputation of all the legit television preachers. He had his work cut out for him. But let's hand it to him, the devil knows what he's doing. The secret? Turns out it was relatively simple. It was just like a cake recipe, he just needed to put all the right ingredients together. And it turned out that the perfect combination was simple. Just mix two parts fame, three parts wealth, one heaping tablespoon of ego, a dash of lust, and bingo! He had his man!

Now that Satan had the bullet, he needed the target. Was it the Christian that was rock solid in his or her faith? Was it the wavering Christian that had an occasional doubt? Was it the generic Christian that just warmed the pew on Sunday morning? Actually, it was none of these. It was *everybody else*! It was the person who wanted to justify why he or she was not interested in Christianity at all. It was the person that needed a world-class excuse, an excuse that nobody could deny. Enter the TV evangelist.

It's the TV evangelist that is raking in millions with his or her plea for donations to *"my ministry with wings"* (also known as a fourteen million dollar Lear jet). The TV evangelist that declared: "If our viewers out there in television land don't send in twenty-five dollars this morning, God is going to call me home tonight!" Or what about the TV evangelist that in the name of prosperity (his prosperity), preaches the poor widow woman out of her last dime? Yes, it could even be the TV evangelist that just got caught having an affair with his, uh...boyfriend. The list goes on. These on-air yahoos have about the same credibility as that of an infomercial host.

Here's the point...I would venture to say that the success of television evangelism has been about a *push*. If the Billy Grahams of the world have led a couple of million people to Christ, the bogus TV evangelists have probably driven about that same number away.

Bottom line—if any of our readers are considering the exciting world of TV evangelism, please remember that you are going to be in a position to affect many lives, one way or the other. Here's a thought I hope we all will consider...imagine the consequences of driving just *one person* away from Christ, not to mention thousands or even millions? Maybe that's why television preachers get the big bucks...because without a doubt, they have the most dangerous job in the world. The rewards can be huge...but the risks can be *hell*.

Discussion Guide

1.   Do you agree with the premise that TV evangelists probably affect the way non-believers view Christianity more any other single entity? _____ If so, in what way do you think

they are affected? Positively or negatively? _____
Please explain:

_____

_____

2.   Who is your favorite TV evangelist?

_____

Why?

_____

3.   Who is your least favorite TV evangelist?

_____

Why?

_____

4.   If you had to guess, what percentage of non-believers
blame their disinterest in Christianity on TV evangelists? _____
What do you think they would say is their biggest "issue" with
TV evangelists?

_____

_____

5.   Here's a tough one...in general, do you think TV
evangelism has resulted in more good or more harm to
Christianity? Check one: More good: _____ More harm: _____
Please explain your choice:

_____

_____

_____

6.   Out of any 10 evangelists that appeared on television this
week, how many do you believe would be trying to sell
something? _____ Do you agree that some T.V. evangelists put
more emphasis on their products than their message? ____ Does
it bother you when that happens? _____ Why or why not?

_____

7.   If you owned a Christian television network, would you make any changes concerning television evangelism? _____ If so, what might those changes be?

_____

_____

8.   What scripture might you suggest a TV evangelist read before going on the air?

_____

_____

_____

Notes:

Chapter
Fifteen

The World Famous "Hypocrite" Excuse

The tension could not have been higher as the National Church Association prepared to crown one "excuse" as the king...the most glamorous and most used excuse out there for dismissing and blowing off Christianity. The contenders were formidable, each and every one was responsible for sending thousands, if not millions of people to (shall we say) a rather warm destination.

The boardwalk of Atlantic City was the perfect choice to hold such an event. As a hotbed of gambling (with your future) and home of the Miss America pageant for decades, AC just felt right. This city seemed a natural to host the "Best Excuse of the 21st Century" competition. And down at the casinos, odds makers were busy putting heavy money on the two favorites...

† "I Don't Want To Go To Church with Hypocrites"

† "But I'm A Good Person, Too."

This was shaking out to be a grudge match of epic proportions, but let's not forget about a fast-closing dark horse. The "A Loving God Wouldn't Send People To Hell" excuse had made some serious inroads in the past half-century, and many predicted it could stage an upset victory. Let the competition begin: The swimsuit segment of the competition was just that...which excuse out there had the most sex appeal? Wow! That's a tough one, what with excuses like "Sunday Is My Only Day Off" and "POP!" which as we all know is an acronym for Party Over Prayer! It should be noted that "POP!" is a new updated name for the old standby "I'm Too Young...I'll Go To Church When I'm Too Old To Have Any More Fun."

And what about the evening gown competition to show off excuses that are the most beautiful? "A Loving God Wouldn't Send People To Hell" was the odds-on favorite to take this category, but a relative newcomer, "Why Come Today, It's Not Even Christmas?" is starting to move up the charts. Seriously, I once told my dad that I wasn't going to church except on Christmas and Easter and he snapped, "Oh, that's just beautiful!" See, it *is* a beautiful excuse!

We interrupt this chapter to bring our readers the following article:

NO EXCUSE SUNDAY

Welcome to "No Excuse Sunday." Next Sunday's service is dedicated to all missing church attendees. To make it possible for everyone to attend church next Sunday, we hereby announce the details of "No Excuse Sunday." Cots will be placed in the foyer for those who say, "Sunday is my only day to sleep in." There will be a special section with lounge chairs for those who feel the pews are too hard. There will be concrete pillows for those who may feel the pews are too soft. Eye drops will be available for those with tired eyes from watching TV late on Saturday night. We will supply steel helmets for those who say, "The roof would cave in if I ever came to church." Blankets will be furnished for those who think the church is too cold and fans for those who say it's too hot. Scorecards will be available for those who wish to keep a tally of the hypocrites present. Relatives and friends will be invited for a fully catered meal afterwards for those who can't attend church and cook lunch, too. We will distribute "Stamp Out Stewardship" buttons for those who feel the church is always asking for money. One section will be decorated with trees, plants and grass for those who like to seek God in nature. Doctors and nurses will be in attendance for those who plan to be sick on Sunday morning. The sanctuary will be decorated with both Christmas poinsettias and Easter lilies for those who have never seen the church without them. And finally, we will provide hearing aids for those who can't hear the preacher and cotton balls for those who think he or she is too loud. Hope to see you there! (This just in...I found the guy who had this article up on his website and he gave me permission to reprint it. Thanks to Ted Terrebonne.)

Meanwhile back at the competition, the judges were casting their final ballots. It was a nail-biter for sure. Just imagine, the number one best excuse in America to avoid Christianity was about to be announced...an excuse that millions upon millions could use. Think of the money it would save them in tithing, think of the Sunday mornings they could sleep in, think of the risqué channels they could watch on TV, think of the internet porn sites they could visit on their computers, think of the suggestive books they could read, think of the Wednesday night bowling they wouldn't have to miss, think, think, think. Ah yes, our excuses, they are a wonderful thing...of sorts.

Finally, it was time for the judges to announce the winner. A deep hush fell over the crowd. The big question was how they would decide which, out of all the wonderful excuses, was the best one...the one that could be used by the most people. And the winner is...drum roll please! "Ladies and gentlemen, the winner of the best excuse of the twenty-first century for blowing off Christianity is the *hypocrite* excuse!" Thunderous applause erupts, shouting and cheering and confetti streaming from the ceiling! It's party time in Atlantic City...and around the world. The hypocrite excuse has finally been fully legitimized! Praise the devil!

So the obvious question is, why did the hypocrite excuse walk away as "Best Excuse of the 21st Century?" It was simple. It's because this excuse is legit! There **are** hypocrites in our churches. When a person invokes this excuse, he or she has every right to do so because it's true. Now don't get me wrong, I'm not saying this excuse gets them off the hook, far from it. But they do have a valid point. And to my knowledge, no one, not one single person in the entire world has ever admitted to being a hypocrite. It's kind of hard to battle a foe that for all intents and purposes doesn't exist. But here's the deal—some of us are hypocrites. And someday, those of us who are must answer for that behavior. It won't be pretty.

Warning! Warning! Incoming! Here comes the "hypocrite excuse!" Be prepared to defend against it. Here's how: If any of us are ever confronted with this excuse, here's my advice. Say to the person, "Yes, there are hypocrites in our church, but we don't go to church to worship hypocrites, we go to worship God." And if this person still has reservations about going to a church full of hypocrites, I would recommend we might share the following with them. It's the best quote I've ever heard concerning hypocrites. It goes something like this: "Hypocrites? Yeah, but you have a choice, you can either go to church with 'em or you can go to hell with 'em. It's up to you."

Discussion Guide

This chapter is not just about the hypocrite excuse; it's about excuses in general. In this discussion, let's take a whole laundry list of excuses and try to develop a response to them. I'll give you the excuse; you give me your response. Here we go:

Excuse #1: *"I don't believe in organized religion."*

_____

_____

Excuse # 2: *"Sunday morning is my only day to sleep."*

_____

Excuse #3: "*You don't have to go to church to be a Christian.*"

Excuse #4: "*I can't believe in a god that allows so much evil.*"

Excuse #5: "*I can't afford all the new clothes it would take.*"

Excuse #6: "*There are lots of religions...how do you know Christianity is the only one that is true?*"

Excuse #7: "*I will wait until I get older.*"

Excuse #8: "*God wouldn't want me, I'm too big of a scumbag.*"

Excuse #9: And finally, do you agree that even we as Christians occasionally use excuses to get us out of doing the Lord's work? _____ If so, feel free to give an example:

Notes:

Chapter Sixteen

The Territorial Christian

When I first told a friend (hey Nancy B) the name of this chapter she said, "Oh, that's when someone makes the mistake of taking your seat in the church pew." I'm afraid it's a little more complicated than that but I will address her statement later in this chapter. First, a touch of history…I used to publish a Christian business directory in a community about fifty miles from my home. Each day I would travel about an hour west to call on prospective clients. And as I crossed into and later exited the next county, there should have been a sign that warned: **"You Are Now Entering/Leaving Your Area of Accountability."** Yes, the sign would work for *both* directions.

This hypothetical sign refers to the fact that some of us Christians have two sets of behavior patterns, depending on our geographic location at the time. I call these individuals "territorial Christians" and they fall into one of two categories. The first is the Christian that may modify his or her behavior once they leave their own hometown. The second is the person that treats another Christian differently knowing that this individual is from another community other than his or her own.

And I suppose most of us are guilty of territorialism to a degree. I have found myself acting a little different when I'm not, as they say, in my own backyard. Why is that? I think it's because no one is there to hold us accountable. No one knows our name, what church we go to, or anything about us. And since they don't know whether we are a Christian or not, evidently some of us don't think we necessarily have to act like one. Maybe we think this anonymity gives us a license to act as we please.

Here are a couple examples of what I'm talking about: First, let me explain that I not only had a Christian business directory in an area west of here; I also have that same publication in my hometown of Panama City. So when I talk about territorial Christian behavior in respect to my occupation, I am comparing apples to apples.

For instance, I might make an appointment to meet someone in a neighboring county. And when I get to our meeting place, usually a McDonalds or Burger King, more times than I care to remember the person I was suppose to meet turns out to be a no-show. I would call their cell phone and get no response. Caller ID is a wonderful thing if we're dodging a bill collector (smiley face goes here) but not so much if avoiding a fellow Christian. Now, if I had been calling on clients in my own hometown, I'm fairly certain the person in question would have had the courtesy to at least either call and cancel or apologize if he or she was unable to keep the appointment.

I also have had more collection problems in communities other than my own. Once again, it all comes down to a matter of accountability. The person that avoided paying the money they owed knew full well they would probably never see me again. I think that's sad, but I'm afraid some of us do it. Yes, even me. I'm feeling convicted even as I type this sentence. It's interesting how we Christians have no problem pointing out the faults of others, but conveniently forget about our own identical behavior. We need to do what a friend of mine calls "man up." That means to face the most embarrassing of situations head on. Face them; deal with them like a man and then move on. Stuff like that would surely make God smile...and we need to be all about making our Creator happy...not that we owe him or anything. Hello!

Now back to my friend's thought that this chapter was about someone having the audacity to take your seat in the church pew. What nerve, huh? Is this also a "territorial" Christian? Well, I suppose of sorts. We treat this as a joke but let's think about it for a moment. What do the un-churched and un-saved fear most about walking into a typical Sunday morning sanctuary? I bet the list is a mile long... "I don't know the words to the hymns"... "I don't have nice enough clothes."... "I don't have money for the collection plate"... and on and on. Can we Christians be partly to blame for keeping folks away from attending a Sunday morning church service? Ya think! Consider the following story...it's not about a territorial Christian in the context of this chapter, but it's about a Christian protecting their "supposed" territory, nonetheless. And unfortunately, it's a true story.

Randy and Kay had put off coming to church for years. It was finally time. They both dreaded going but knew from their upbringing that it was the thing to do. Finally they got up the nerve. Kay went out and bought about three hundred dollars worth of Sunday-go-to-meeting clothes. Randy took his funeral suit to the dry-cleaners. The dreaded Sunday morning finally arrived and the couple got in the car and headed to church. Randy tried to do a one-eighty about fourteen times but the wife threatened to smack him. They arrived a few minutes early. Let the festivities begin...

"Hello, how are you this beautiful Sunday morning?" the usher asked as he welcomed the nervous pair. "Hmmm, so far so good," Kay thought to herself. They were among the first to arrive so naturally they got their choice of seats. A front row seat was available. In fact, the first two rows offered the best seats in the house. So naturally, since Randy and Kay were there bright and early, they got their pick of the seats...in the very *back pew*!

As Kay was reading over the bulletin, Randy noticed the congregation members were beginning to file in. It was almost as if there was assigned seating. Each individual, couple or family walked in and headed straight to what appeared to be their own *personal* seat. "What is this?" Randy asked himself, "a football stadium? Would the man in aisle eight, row three, seat sixteen please return to the stadium parking lot? You've left your lights on." He then chuckled to himself and began reading announcements on the overhead projector. Then it happened…

"Excuse me," the rather un-amused looking matronly lady huffed, "you're in our seats."

"Pardon me?" Randy asked with a confused look on his face.

"These are our seats," the lady explained in a rather arrogant manner, "we have been sitting here for thirty-five years."

Randy looked around. There must have been a hundred and fifty empty seats. His face turned red, he was embarrassed and just a touch on the peeved side.

Kay whispered to Randy, "Let's move."

"To a different seat?" Randy asked.

"No," Kay said, *"to a different address."*

It took three more years for Randy and Kay to get up the nerve to try church again.

Discussion Guide

1.   According to what you read in this chapter, how would you define a territorial Christian?

_____

_____

_____

2.   Do you agree that many of us Christians probably act "territorial" from time to time? _____ If so, why do you think that is?

_____

3.   Do you ever recall a time when you acted differently being out of your "territory?" No answer is necessary, but if anyone wants to lay it out there, be our guest:

_____

_____

4.   Case Study: You are sitting in a Burger King having lunch (this is a stretch, huh?) when a well-dressed woman approaches your table. She says that she is a little embarrassed to ask, but she noticed your Christian t-shirt and assumed you were a believer. She tells you that she, too, is a believer. She explains that her church, which is across town, is having a fund-raiser for the local elderly population. She is selling raffle tickets for $10 each. This is a chance to win a weekend at the beach. You know full well that if it were your church, you would probably buy five tickets. But this isn't your church. You decline to buy any tickets. That being said, is it possible that sometimes we even act territorial within our own community? _____ Will we support our own church but neglect the opportunity to assist a neighboring church or church member? _____ If so, why do you think we act this way?

_____

_____

_____

_____

5.   Does the Bible actually say that we are to do good to all men, but especially to fellow believers? Check one: Yes: ____ No: ____ I have no clue: ____ (tiny little hint: Gal. 6:10)

Notes:

CHAPTER SEVENTEEN

Are Some of Us Too "Christianized?"

I relate the following from personal experience. After studying the Bible for a few years, I felt I was beginning to lose touch with the secular world. It was becoming hard for me to carry on even the simplest of conversations with a non-believer...and that's a terrible thing. Yes, I was alienating possible new Christians with my "foreign tongue." This exotic language is referred to by the secular world as "bible babble." How in the world are we going to witness to someone who can't understand a word we're saying? Yes, that might be a bit of an exaggeration, but hopefully I make my point. Yes, I was one of the ones becoming too Christianized. By the way, that simply means becoming too *religious* to relate to the secular world.

Let me give an actual example. About five years after getting saved, I invited one of those "will work for food" dudes to come spend a few days in our home. Actually, we had a little apartment out back and he stayed there. In exchange for food and shelter, he did some of the fun chores. You know, like cleaning the potty and picking up those little brown gifts our new puppy left on the carpet. Anyway, I could tell by the way he was dressed and smelled that he certainly wasn't a Christian. Seriously, a believer doesn't smell like a three-day-old trout that never quite made it to the ice chest. Excuse me! I can just hear some of our readers asking: "Do you honestly believe that we can tell by the way a person is dressed and how they smell as to whether or not they're a Christian?" Well, of course we can! Especially if we have a bad case of the TCS...Too Christianized Syndrome! Our discernment and uncanny ability to judge others just comes naturally to those of us that have elevated ourselves to the ranks of the "super-saved."

Now back to my story. So I decide this homeless heathen needs a little Jesus. In fact, he needed a whole Bible full of Jesus! So I start out by asking him about his spiritual life. He responded that he once had an out-of-body experience after doing some bad LSD and knocking back about two cases of Miller Genuine Draft. I rolled my eyes (eye-rolling is a sure sign of the super-saved) and explained to him that I was talking about God, does he believe in God? "Of course I believe in God," he tells me, "and I also believe in miracles."

As he explained to me, that "miracle stuff" was because he had heard football superstar Joe Namath guarantee a victory in the 1969 Super Bowl. He then watched as Broadway Joe and his upstart Jets took down the mighty Baltimore Colts in the greatest upset in NFL history. "What a miracle!" he exclaimed. I responded to him with the most self-righteous eye-roll that I had in my arsenal.

Since I had established (of sorts) that he believed in God, I took it to the next level. Does he know who Jesus and the Holy Spirit are? This is where I thought I might lose him. How did I know? Well, because this time he rolled his eyes! "That's easy," he responded, "Jesus is the main dude in the Bible." So I followed up by asking, "And the Holy Ghost, are you filled with the Holy Ghost?" And he responded, "The holy what? Make up your mind dude, is it spirit or ghost?" So I began my explanation of the Trinity. He responded by yawning and telling me he used to date a girl named Trinity in the third grade. I could tell I was getting nowhere.

Getting nowhere, huh? That's where a lot of us are getting when we try to communicate with seekers or non-believers. Especially if we use words they might not understand. Words like *anointed, trinity, justified, sanctified, glorified, transfiguration, stewardship* and many, many others.

I remember an Alpha class that I led. As you may recall from an earlier chapter, an Alpha class is a "non-churchy" way to introduce folks to Christ. We were dealing with some individuals that had no clue about Christianity. And one of the attendees was this wonderful older gentleman, Thomas Henderson. He was an old-school mechanic who was about as salt-of-the-earth as they come. But I could tell he really wanted to understand what this "church thang" (as he put it) was all about.

We were having a discussion about the crucifixion. So I spoke for about thirty minutes on that subject, the very heart of Christianity. I then asked Thomas to paraphrase what I had just said. I should have seen his response coming. He started out by asking, "What's a paraphrase?" When I explained that I wanted him to summarize what I had been teaching on for the past half hour, he simply said, "Oh, that's easy…Jesus lived, he croaked on the cross for our sins and he'll be back." Amazing! Thomas said in one sentence what it took me thirty minutes to dance around. You talk about cutting to the chase! Thomas did exactly that.

So why in the world do some of us Christians have to make it so complicated? Uh, hello me! And why do some of us feel we have to show off all our Bible knowledge when witnessing to the lost? Not only is it not necessary, it's not effective. It's really quite simple… "Jesus lived, he croaked on the cross for our sins and he'll be back." End of story.

Discussion Guide

1.   Have you ever known a person that made you think to yourself: "Wow, I hope this dude doesn't think he or she will win any folks to Christ with that know-it-all attitude or demeanor?" _____ If so, without naming names, please explain:

_____

_____

_____

2.   After reading Chapter 17 and in your own words, what is the definition of a person that may be too "Christianized?"

_____

_____

_____

3.   Do you find that the longer you are a Christian, the harder it is to relate to the non-believer? _____ If so, why do you think that is?

_____

_____

_____

4.   Is it possible that one of Satan's tools is to give us a self-righteous attitude? _____ Is it also possible that the longer we are Christians, the more we become judgmental concerning the unsaved and un-churched? _____ What are some practical ways to defend ourselves against such attitudes?

_____

_____

_____

5.   What are just a few of the words that we might avoid when witnessing in order not to appear too Christianized?

_____

_____

_____

6.   Have you ever been in a small group or Sunday school class where someone always made it known that he or she knew the most scripture? _____ No name calling, we've probably all done it. In your opinion, might this be an early symptom of becoming too Christianized? _____ Why or why not?

_____

_____

_____

_____

Notes:

CHAPTER EIGHTEEN

The Sunday Herd

It's seven minutes after twelve on a Sunday afternoon and all hell is about to break loose. Waiters are negotiating to get out of serving in section four, waitresses are battening down the hatches in preparation for Hurricane Herd, and busboys are taking their last cigarette break before the category five storm hits.

Yes, "they" are on the way. They come by the hundreds. They are dressed up all pretty. They demand priceless service. They drink water to save a buck or they ask for ten packs of lemon juice to make their own lemonade. They leave with about five of those little coffee creamer thingies stuffed into their pockets, not to mention the fourteen packs of *Splenda*. They did not order black-eyed peas...they ordered white acre peas! They think their waiter has forgotten all about them. They seem oblivious to the fact that their three little crumb crunchers are screaming louder than a squadron of incoming F-16 fighter jets.

Their coffee is too hot! Their coffee is too cold! Their coffee is too just right! They have a fly in their soup! Well, pieces of pepper should not be ground so large, a big piece looks just like a fly! They attack the all-you-can-eat buffet with a vengeance! They leave with a purse full of fried chicken. They justify this little indiscretion by calling it a "doggie purse." They keep the table occupied for what seems like forever… my daughter tells me the wait staff refers to this practice not so lovingly as "camping." They order "one last Coke" which sets a new restaurant refill record at *twenty-seven*.

Finally, they leave. Oh, thank heaven for 7-11. The busboy arrives. There it is, lying next to the peppershaker. It's a tip. No wait, that's not a tip, it's one quarter and two pathetic little pennies. But hey, the meal total was over one hundred dollars! Are you kidding me! That's not a tip, that's an insult! Their waiter follows them to their car. "Here mister, you probably need this more than I do! Add another quarter to it and you can make a phone call!" And that, my friends, is why "they" are known not so affectionately in restaurant circles as the "Sunday Herd."

Sally is a new waitress at the restaurant. "So, Joey, how did you know they were part of the herd?" she asks her busboy. "Three things," he responds, "they arrive like a herd of charging bulls, they are completely oblivious to the fact that their server is waiting on about ten other tables simultaneously and finally, what they call a tip is what we refer to as chump change!"

Would it be fair to say that the above is an exaggeration? Yes and no. The behavior of the vast majority of Christians can't be associated with the Sunday Herd. On the other hand, a few of us Christians out there are probably guilty as charged. And if we have ever acted in the way described above, then congratulations, someday we too may be inducted into the "Herd of Fame."

But here is some good news…you know how we Christians are taught that others are constantly observing our lives? Well, I think this presents a grand opportunity right under our hungry faces. Members of wait staffs are constantly observing and making judgment calls concerning their customers. That can't be said of most other work environments in our society. As a customer, we are under the microscope from the minute we walk into a restaurant until the time we depart. So let your light shine! Treat your waiter or waitress like they are the most important person in the world. Treat them as if they were your very own daughter, son, brother or sister. Give them something that waitresses and waiters seldom get...RESPECT! If we do, we not only are separating ourselves from the herd, we are setting ourselves up to get that priceless service we talked about earlier...and guess what? Priceless service might inspire us to offer more generous tips, which could speak volumes to our servers about the kind of people we are.

And here's the kicker... maybe, just maybe, because we are so refreshing to our servers, they might want to know more about us. Hey, they might want to be more like us. In fact, they might even want to get to know us better because we are so "different"...in a good way. Perhaps this is our opening, our opportunity to tell them about somebody that changed our lives and might even change theirs. Just tell them it has something to do with a guy named J.C. I'm pretty sure the Holy Spirit can take it from there.

By the way, Jesus left the best tip of all... "I am the way, the truth and the life!" And you can take that to the eternal bank!

Discussion Guide

1.   Case Study: You and your family have been seated next to a large group for Sunday lunch. Both parties have the same waitress. She has been very attentive to both tables. When you first sat down you noticed the other group blessing their meal as their waitress waited patiently to serve their drinks. After the meal, the other party of about eight people exited the restaurant. Apparently they did not leave a tip as the young lady asked the bus boy if he had picked it up. You had observed that no tip was left on the table (and for this study, we will state as fact that no tip was left on a credit card). What do you think about such behavior?

_____

_____

2.   Do you believe it is possible for a waiter or waitress to form an opinion concerning Christianity based solely on the behavior of their customers? _____ Why or why not?

_____

_____

3.   What scripture might you suggest to help us with our behavior in public? _____
Please paraphrase the scripture:

_____

_____

4.   Have you or your family ever observed "Sunday Herd" type behavior while at a restaurant? _____ Please elaborate:

_____

_____

5.   If you could give one piece of advice to each Christian before they enter a restaurant after church on Sunday afternoon, what would it be?

_____

_____

6.   Do you think that a sermon specifically on "restaurant etiquette for Christians" would be appropriate? _____ Why or why not?

_____

_____

Chapter Nineteen

The Harry Potter Syndrome

I have a friend who under no circumstances would ever let her kids read a Harry Potter book. The magic, the spells, the fairy dust, the boiling pot of witches' brew...not to mention the two-hundred zillion books sold to a worldwide audience. So I asked my friend, "How come you are so against the Harry Potter books?"

She replied, "Because they are so anti-Christian." So naturally, I asked her if she had read them. "Of course not." she explained. "Then how do you know they are so anti-Christian?" I continued. "Because my sister told me!" she snapped. I could tell she was getting a little miffed at this point but I had to know. "I assume she's read them?" "Not in this lifetime!" she barked, "She wouldn't read that kind of trash!"

But keep in mind, that very same friend forwards me "those" emails. You know what I'm talking about; you've seen gazillions of them. The emails that describe in detail the "true story" of how a big white, glowing, 7-foot angel took down a pack of pinheads as they were about to gang rape a young crippled woman in New York City's Central Park. By the way, I believe in angels, just not the "made up by someone's imagination" kind. And most of us probably remember this one:

"The Dell Computer company will send you a free laptop if you forward this to ten of your friends." And let's not forget about the "forward this and you will receive a large financial blessing by 4 o'clock tomorrow afternoon." Are you kidding me! Engaging in this type of behavior makes some of us look like a bunch of gullible pinheads.

And therein lays my theory: some of us Christians take stands against or promote things of which we *knoweth* not. Now, don't get me wrong, I'm no big fan of the Potter books. Hey, there you go! I just proved my own theory. You see, I haven't read any of the Potter books either, and here I am deciding that I don't care for them based on a little second-hand gossip.

To the secular world, when we make a judgment or spread propaganda based on nothing more than a feeling or hearsay, in their eyes we substantially weaken our ability to make the case for Christ. We might hear them responding to our foolish behavior by saying something like: "Hey, those Christians will believe anything!" Or maybe: "Hey bible-thumpers, I have some awesome ocean front property in Kansas for sale as soon as the tide goes out!" Here's the point…should the secular world believe us about events that happened over two thousand years ago when we can't even get our facts straight about something that happened only twenty minutes ago?

I have a suggestion. The next time we get one of "those" emails, before we dare forward it, let's go to *www.snopes.com* and check it out. The sole purpose of this website is to chase down rumors, wild claims, etc., and differentiate between fact and fiction. And believe it or not, a stunning three or four percent of the time, the email content is *actually true*. Okay, okay, two percent of the time!

In conclusion, we need to remember that some in the secular world would like nothing more than to see us Christians portray ourselves as gullible. So the next time we stake out a position on something, whether it be the Harry Potter books, Halloween, that photo-shopped cloud that looks like the fingers of God or even my favorite myth that Santa Claus is coming to town, let's make sure we know what we are talking about. People respect facts, not fiction. By the way, if there are any elves listening out there, I promise that I have been a very good boy this year! Maybe you-know-who will bring me a Harry Potter book.

Discussion Guide

1.   Case Study: Your new mother-in-law, who is a devout Christian, tells you not to plant a pecan tree in her backyard because it is Sunday. According to her, a pecan tree (or any tree for that matter) will not bear fruit if planted on the Lord's Day. At the time, you are a non-believer. Could a statement like this possibly affect the way you view Christians? _____ Why or why not?

_____

_____

_____

Footnote: *The above is a true story. My mother-in-law, Dorothy Mason (God rest her sweet soul) told me one Sunday afternoon in 1967 that I better wait until Monday to plant the tree. She explained why. However, over 40 years later this pecan tree is one of the most prolific fruit bearing trees in all of Alabama.*

2.   Do you agree that some of us Christians occasionally say things when we really don't know what we're are talking about? _____ Do you agree that we, of all people, should guard against saying things with a reckless disregard of the facts? _____ Why is that so important?

_____

_____

3.   Case Study: Janet, a born again Christian, was inviting all her friends over to her home to hear about an "*amazing new*

product." It could heal diabetes, make you live 40 years longer, make you look 40 years younger and it could even grow hair on a cue ball. It was some good stuff! At least that's what Janet read in the sales brochure and she was regurgitating it out verbatim. There was only one tiny little problem. As the group would soon found out, the product was bogus. Three weeks later she was attempting to witness to one of the attendees. Is it possible that Janet may have lost some of her credibility?

_____

_____

_____

_____

Notes:

Chapter Twenty

A Big Fat "No!"

My wife is a prayer intercessor. For those of you who might not know what that means, she intercedes for others with prayers to God. It is a special calling that she was very blessed to receive. Praying for others is one of the most selfless things we can do, and I'm thinking it really makes God smile. However, in some instances there may be a problem.

I hope my wife doesn't read this chapter. I will probably just tear it out and say that Putters or Puglsey ate it. Putters is my daughter Danielle's Pekingese. Pugsley is my daughter Brandy's pug. We also have another pug named Smoke. That's my daughter Marlenna's dog. Smoke doesn't eat book chapters; he eats two-dollar fancy shoes from retailer K-Martini…which is the designer section of K-Mart. We also have a dog named Randy Averett but that's another story. Anyway, back to the potential problem with a type of prayer.

There are basically two types of prayer, *public* and *private*. A private prayer is just between God and us with no other individuals present. On the other hand, a public prayer can be defined as any prayer where there are two or more people present.

Here is an interesting side note that has nothing whatsoever to do with this chapter. I once heard a person say that God probably preferred public prayers over private prayers. Why? His reasoning was that in public prayer, we are probably less selfish. In that type of prayer, we tend to put the needs of others over that of ourselves. On the other hand, with the prayer just between us and our Creator, he suggested we may find ourselves presenting God with a whole laundry list of "stuff" that we want. Not always, but sometimes.

Here's an idea if you ever have a slow moment in your Sunday school class or small group. Ask the participants which prayer they think God might prefer, *public* or *private*. I can promise that someone will draw a line in the sand and you will end up having a rather lively and interesting discussion. I call discussions like that "stirring up the pot" because invariably they do just that. But since this typically takes place in a Sunday school class or small group, seldom does a full-blown fistfight break out.

So here we are in this hospital room and my wife, Vicki, decides it's time to pray for our friend. Since there are several people present, including Jack, the non-believing roommate, this is one of those public prayers I mentioned earlier. Our friend had recently been diagnosed with a brain tumor. Vicki and I are no strangers to that diagnosis, as our daughter Marlenna was diagnosed with a massive "lemon size" brain tumor in July of 2007. And by the way, after three huge miracles and a bunch of average-sized miracles, Marlenna is completely healed. Thanks for asking; now back to the public prayer. As best I remember, the prayer for our friend went something like this:

"Dear Father God, we come to you today in the name of Jesus Christ. Our sister and your child Dottie (not her real name) has been diagnosed with a very serious illness. Father, we know you are the Great Physician and ask that you, in your infinite power and wisdom and according to your perfect will, heal our sister. Your word says that if two or more are gathered in your name, you are there. And your word also says that you will heal and protect your children. We stand on that promise and claim her healing. We thank you, Father; we know you are in full control of Dottie's life and we know you will heal her according to your perfect will. We thank you for being a Holy God, a God that loves his children. Thank you for loving and healing our sister in Christ. In the matchless and precious name of Jesus Christ, we pray. Amen."

The next week I arrived at Dottie's room. Her bed was empty. Jack saw me enter and in what sounded like an almost sarcastic tone said, "Well, it looks like your wife's prayer was answered with a big, fat *no!*" To Jack, that was exactly how it appeared. Vicki prayed for our friend's healing and she died. As a Christian, we know that Jack did not understand. Yes, as a matter of fact, God did answer Vicki's prayer. Dottie received "perfect healing" according to His will. She passed from this life to a life of perfect health, of perfect everything.

Here's my point: sometimes we Christians can set ourselves up for failure in the eyes of the non-believer. All Jack heard was Vicki claiming a one hundred percent healing from God. But in his eyes she was not healed. Period, end of story! If she had been, she would not have died. Jack missed and probably wouldn't understand the part about Vicki asking that God's *perfect will* be done. And it was...God answered her prayer by ending our friend's suffering and pain on this earth and bestowed upon her his gift of "perfect healing." But not to Jack, he heard Vicki ask for healing and our friend passed away. And as far as Jack was concerned, that was the end of the discussion.

I have heard numerous public prayers just like Vicki's. And I'm sure there have been many non-believers who've overheard similar prayers and then waited suspiciously for the outcome. If the results weren't positive in their eyes, it provided them with just "one more reason" to doubt. But what if those public prayers were re-worded just a tad when non-believers are present? Something that would let the non-believer realize that death for a child of God is not a "*big fat no*" but quite the contrary, it is the ultimate healing.

For starters, what if we incorporated something like the following phrase into our public prayers...especially if we think a non-believer is within earshot? "God we know you answer all prayers, and we understand that you answer them in different ways. We know that sometimes you answer with a 'yes,' sometimes with a 'no,' sometimes with a 'wait,' and maybe even sometimes with 'I've got a better idea.'"

This simple phrase added to a prayer may let the non-believer know that we as Christians don't expect God to always give us exactly what we want. No earthly father has ever done that and I'm quite sure God the Father isn't going to buck the trend now. Hey, if he gave my daughters all the "stuff" they have prayed for over the years, he would be out of stuff by now!

That reminds me of a joke: So our president calls me on the phone the other day and says, "Bobby, have your wife and three daughters go shopping this weekend." I ask, "Why?" and the president answers, "Because it would provide a jump-start to the national economy!" Okay, okay, I didn't say it was a funny joke.

When we are praying in the presence of non-believers concerning a life or death matter, I feel we should somehow explain (for the benefit of the non-believer's ears) that the "death" answer is not necessarily a "no" answer. Maybe we could include a phrase something like the following in our prayer: "Father God, you know that we love so-in-so and would hate to see them leave us. But Father, we also know what awaits your children in heaven. Because of our selfishness, if it were up to us we would keep so-and-so many more years here on earth. However, we know that is your decision, not ours. We certainly will never question your wisdom and compassion for your children. Therefore Father, we commit so and so into your hands. Like the old television show, we know that our Father Knows Best."

In conclusion, I think that if we will consider how the non-believer may interpret our prayers and then pray accordingly, our conversations with God might go from having a possible negative effect to a most positive and eternal effect. Just think, we might even walk into a hospital room someday, find that the person we prayed for has gone on to be with the Lord and hear a roommate like Jack say: "Hey, just thought you might like to know that last night God answered your prayers with a big fat *yes!*"

Discussion Guide

You have all heard of "Date Night" but how about "Debate Day?" Well congratulations, that's what today is…the first annual "Debate Day" for your Sunday school class or small group. Here's how it works: First, divide the members into 2 groups and choose leaders. You can even choose a name for your group…if it's the *Christians* vs. *Lions*, let the other team be the Christians. We all know how that one turned out. Okay, after reading the question, each team has 5 minutes to formulate an answer (someone needs to pretend to be an egg timer). The leader of the group shall select the person he or she wishes to present their case. God will decide the winner of the debate so you guys will have to wait until you get to heaven to find out who won. Remember, you have 5 minutes to prepare your answer and up to 5 minutes to present your case. Okay, here we go:

1. A non-believer asks your team why it appears as if some people are healed when prayed for and some are not. To this non-believer it seems as if healing is just the luck of the draw. How would your team respond to this person?

2. A non-believer asks your team to provide scripture to prove that God not only hears prayers, but he answers them. Please provide scripture and commentary.

3. According to a premise in Chapter 20, when saying a prayer in public, it is suggested that the person praying

should be mindful of any non-believers present. Does your team agree with that premise and why or why not?

4. Just for grins, have one team take the "pro" and one the "con" side of the following statement: Some people think because they are usually more selfless, God prefers *public* prayers over *private* prayers. (Have a coin toss to see which teams argues "pro" and which team argues "con").

Footnote: *The author realizes that no one knows but God how he views prayer, but I think it is healthy to discuss our prayer life. After all, communication with God is what it's all about.*

Notes:

Chapter Twenty One

Chasing Rabbits
and Howard Stern

I vividly recall the Sunday morning in 1998 when I chased my first rabbit. I didn't know I was chasing rabbits, but evidently I was. And I certainly did not know there was an unspoken rule that we were not supposed to chase rabbits. In case you aren't familiar, these rabbits aren't the kind that eat carrots and do Easter. No, these rabbits are actual *discussion topics* concerning Christianity.

For instance, if your Sunday school class is discussing the Old Testament prophets and someone asks if the class believes Judas Iscariot is in hell, that question could be considered chasing a rabbit. It is a legitimate question but if it is not directly related to the discussion at hand, someone in the class may accuse the person that brought up this subject of chasing a rabbit. In the presence of some people, you could get drawn and quartered for such an offense. Yes, these folks may have been interested in a particular rabbit chasing subject earlier in their Christian journey, but as they matured in Christ, they became less willing to go on the chase.

My rabbit was the *Catholic faith.* I was chasing it about a year after the "Howard Stern" incident. Oh, I haven't mentioned that, have I? Yes, I had an argument with Howard on a national radio broadcast that ultimately led to my accepting Christ. What! God used that shock-jock to bring someone to Christ? No way! Way! If you don't mind, we shall chase the Howard Stern rabbit for a moment or two. Here are the Cliff Notes of my testimony:

I mentioned in an earlier chapter about my risqué newspaper called *Beach Bull* that Satan and I founded in 1990. My lifestyle as publisher of the Bull was just a snitch on the disgusting side as I spent the next few years divorcing my wife, gambling, getting ripped and in general, just living a life of debauchery.

Then one day in the fall of 1996, I received a phone call from a local radio station. They had bought the syndicated Howard Stern Show and needed a "generic" celebrity to officially welcome him and his show to the local market. I was offered the opportunity, and gladly accepted. I had a secret agenda that you will understand in a few minutes.

As some of you may remember, October of '96 was a fine time in the life of baseball fans, especially Atlanta Brave fans. The Braves were in the World Series and had traveled to the Big Apple to whip up on the mighty Yankees. Atlanta dominated in the first two games of the series, 12 to1 and 4 to 0. And I know some of you guys won't believe this, but Yankee fans don't take it lightly when a team, especially a Southern team, comes to town and puts a hurtin' on their boys! We're talking booing, hissing, throwing cups and even tossing an occasional hamburger...of course, if you've ever attempted to eat a burger at Yankee stadium, you will understand that pitching them onto the field is completely justifiable. I've eaten tastier hockey pucks. But back to the fan behavior, I found it to be a bit on the rude side.

Fast-forward to the big day, the Howard Stern Show in all his glory was coming to the Florida Panhandle…and I was laying in wait. The media were all there including the local newspaper and various affiliated radio stations. The big moment arrived and the local announcer proclaimed: "And now ladies and gentlemen, we cut live to New York City and the world-famous Howard Stern Show!

Time out while I give you some background. Since this incident happened many years ago, I decided to go down to the local library and look up on microfilm the newspaper article that appeared in our local paper concerning the Stern incident. Since my memory of the event and the newspaper article differed somewhat, in the interest of accuracy, I will report what happened according to the printed article. The story did say however, that much of what was said on-air could not be printed in a family newspaper. Okay, here we go:

When it was my turn at the microphone, instead of welcoming him and his show to the area, I reminded Howard that the Braves were putting a whipping on his Yankees and that I couldn't decide who was ruder, folks from New York or New Jersey. Well, Howard was quick to respond by saying and I quote: "The rudest person on the planet is your mother who raised you and gave you such a foul mouth." As I recall, he also directed some other comments at my mother but since they weren't in the article, I won't go down that road. But regardless, his comments didn't bother me one bit until…

The very next morning, as I said before, there was a page 2 article in our local daily newspaper, the News Herald. It had a big picture of me in front of the microphone and the quote from Howard that my mother was the rudest person on the planet for raising me with such a foul mouth. That is the morning that if I had been suicidal, I would have blown my brains out. My Christian mother, who was the absolute sweetest, genteel southern woman to ever draw a breath, was humiliated. Several of her friends were nice enough to bring the article to her attention. It was by far the most embarrassing day of my life...and hers. I sincerely wanted to die, but was too afraid to pull the trigger. In retrospect, I'm glad I didn't have the guts, because that would have resulted in a free, all expense paid, one-way ticket to hell, with or without the hand basket.

Enter God into the picture. As you might have guessed, God had been busy behind the scenes orchestrating this entire situation. He knew what it would take to get my attention. He had tried before when he helped me bankrupt Marlenna Fashions, my multi-million dollar apparel business. Unfortunately, I paid him no attention. But when I humiliated my wonderful mother, well, that did it...God had my full and undivided attention.

I remember that morning well. As God would have it, we had recently moved our Beach Bull office from Panama City Beach to downtown Panama City. Our office was now smack dab in the middle of what I referred to as a "nest of Christians." So I walked into work that day and here were all these folks walking around smiling and laughing. They acted as if they didn't have a care in the world. And I recall thinking to myself: "I don't have a clue what these people have, but I want some of it."

Enter Randy McInvale. I considered Randy the leader of this "nest" of Christians. He explained to me that my life was pretty much going down the toilet because I was running the show. He suggested I give God a shot. Randy began witnessing to me, and about four months later (February 27, 1997) on the back steps of the office complex, I turned the Bobby Weaver Show over to Christ. If it weren't for Randy McInvale and the Holy Spirit, this boy would still be headed south. I can never thank God enough for sending Randy my way...you talk about changing an eternal destination!

I have always imagined seeing Jesus that morning as he watched Randy lead me in saying the sinner's prayer. I can just see him wiping his brow and saying to himself: "Wow! This is gonna be a challenge!" And believe me, if he did say that, he was spot on! I came with more baggage than an over-booked Delta flight. And with my luck, none of it was lost in Atlanta. Now *that* is a miracle!

Did I mention that a few years back I had divorced my wife? Yes, my Christian wife. Did I mention that a few years back I had broken the hearts of my three young daughters? Yes, and two of those daughters had accepted Christ. Did I mention that I was a major league scumbag? And God took me back in spite of all that. Talk about amazing grace!

Then God got busy. First, he began chipping away at my sins. I'm thinking he used one of those jackhammers from a road building crew...went through a lot of drill bits no doubt. I've managed to hold on to as many sins as I can. After all, they are my babies; I've raised them since childhood. But slowly and surely, God is taking them. And in the meantime, guess what! He put my wife and me back together. Yes, Vicki and I gave divorce our best shot... but it just didn't work out.

I will absolutely never forget the Christmas morning of 2001. I met all four of the girls at my ex-wife's house to open Christmas presents. I asked that they all gather around and open their gifts simultaneously. I am getting tears in my eyes just typing this stuff. All of a sudden there was a collective gasp from my daughters...they hadn't seen it coming! It was a wedding invitation that read something to the effect of: "If You Aren't Too Busy On Or About The 20th Of July of 2002, Your Attendance At Your Parent's Re-Marriage Ceremony Would Be Greatly Appreciated." Screams! Hugs! And the most important thing...Jesus was now running the show. It was the most wonderful moment of my life! My girls were absolutely beside themselves. And Vicki? Hey, she got me back...but she was happy in spite of that!

And the story has one more surprising twist. About two years later, I was sitting at home one evening and the phone rings. It was Marlenna, our oldest daughter. She was calling from Orlando where she lived and worked. She simply said, "Hey

Dad, I said the prayer tonight." Being dumb me I asked, "What prayer?" "You know, Dad, the *prayer*. I accepted Jesus tonight." After about fifteen minutes of yelling and praising God, the celebration finally started to die down. Then it occurred to me...the trifecta was complete! My entire family was not only reunited but all five of us had accepted Jesus Christ as our Lord and Savior. Like the beer commercial said, "It just don't get any better than that!"

Now, with my testimony complete it's time to chase one last rabbit. As I was saying earlier, I remember those early days after accepting Christ. It was an exciting time to study and learn more about Christianity, and I had about a gazillion questions. Unfortunately, I didn't realize that the more mature Christians already had those same questions...about twenty years earlier. And some of them were in no mood to go over the same stuff again.

In fact, still unknown to her, one of the members of my Sunday school class almost ended my Christian career before it really got started. It seems one day that I was "at it again" as some of my classmates described my constant question-asking habit. And out of the blue, one gal spoke up in a less than friendly tone and said, "Let's quit chasing rabbits and get on with our study!" It was like slapping me in the face! And although I never told anyone why, I did not return to that Sunday school class for almost three years. But here's the point of this chapter: I'm afraid there may be some seekers or new Christians out there that might have never returned.

We all go off on tangents now and again. But when a seeker or new Christian goes down that road, I firmly believe we all need to be as tolerant a possible. If we aren't, it's like saying: "We all know there's no such thing as a stupid question...but that's a stupid question."

Maybe we should all try to remember that four seemingly innocuous little words like "Let's quit chasing rabbits" could discourage, if not entirely derail, a person's walk with

Christ…and that's one train wreck I don't think any of us want to be responsible for.

Discussion Guide

1.   Please share with the group your definition of "chasing rabbits." Hint: …and we ain't talking Energizer.

_____

_____

_____

2.   Do you agree that some of us more "mature in Christ" believers can be a little less receptive to chasing rabbits than relatively new believers? _____ Can you see where that might cause friction in a small group or Sunday school class? _____ Please elaborate:

_____

_____

_____

3.   Case Study: Your class or small group is involved in a study of the book of Joshua in the Old Testament. Toward the end of the session, someone asks the group if they mind giving her some advice concerning a personal problem that has come up at work. Ms. Poe, who is leading the study, suggests that a personal issue is similar to rabbit chasing and should be discussed after class, not during. Do you agree with the leader's remarks? _____ Why or why not?

_____

_____

_____

_____

A female member of the group takes issue with the leader, stating that the whole purpose of Bible study is to learn how to apply those principals in everyday life. She felt that if the personal problem was addressed after class, several members of the group might not have time to stay, thus possibly eliminating some valuable input. What is your opinion concerning this situation?

_____

_____

_____

_____

Notes:

Chapter Twenty Two

A Raisin in the Rice Pudding

If it has been said once, it has been said 37 million times: "Eleven o'clock on Sunday morning is the most segregated hour in America." How sad is that? I remember about nine years ago when we were starting an outreach at our church called Loaves & Fishes, we were to go into low-income housing developments to feed the less fortunate. There was a mixed ethnicity that included a large African-American population. This ministry would ultimately last about five years and provide over 250,000 thousand sack lunches. No doubt God blessed this outreach project big-time!

However, as Loaves & Fishes was just getting started, one member of our church approached the founder of the ministry and warned: "If you aren't careful, they are going to start wanting to come to our church; then what you gonna do?"

God forbid! Black people in our church, somebody call in the SWAT team! And here's the wonderful part, the warning was *right on!*

Some of the finest, most spirit-filled folks you will ever meet have joined our church as a result of the Loaves & Fishes ministry. Folks like Miss Emma "Granny" Jordan, Karreen "Dee" Adams, Celestine "I saw her on the Food Channel" Mally, and many more. I call these wonderful ladies the "church spark plugs" and if you were ever to attend our contemporary service, also known as the "Honky Tonk" service, you would understand why. Us white folks are getting a real lesson in worship from our soul sisters...and loving every minute of it! And here's another bonus...with several soul brothers and/or sisters worshipping in our sanctuary, the congregation will never, and I mean never, be characterized as being part of the *frozen chosen!*

Thanks in part to the above warning from a fellow church member; my goal for Forest Park United Methodist is to ultimately become known as America's first "gray" church. I define a gray church as one that has a ratio of blacks and whites similar to that of the population of the United States. So the question becomes, what does having a gray church have to do with our Christian behavior and how it affects new believers? I'll try to answer that.

If we walk into the typical W.A.S.P (White Anglo-Saxon Protestant) church on any given Sunday morning, it will most likely look like a sea of white...or all *salt* and no *pepper*. Now tell me, is that representative of real life in America? Of course it's not! America is the melting pot of the world and people of every ethnicity and color have migrated to our great nation.

If we walk into any grocery store, we get a fair representation of the ethnic fabric of America...a little white, a little black, a little red, a little yellow and various color blends. If we walk into a doctor's office, we get that same fair representation. Hey, even if we walk into the member's only clubhouse of Augusta National, home of the Masters Golf Tournament, we will see a better cross section of America's people than we will in a typical Sunday morning protestant church sanctuary. Some of our readers may be asking themselves, "So what's so bad about that?" Well, for one thing, I think attending a totally segregated church may cause us to miss out on some incredible worship and cultural experiences. Maybe I can give you some examples that will help explain my point. And for the sake of argument, let's assume we are talking about an *all-white* church.

First, in some all-white churches, it's hard to tell the difference between a worship service and a funeral service. I wonder how many of us have ever been to a funeral service in an all black church. I have. You talk about a celebration! It sounded more like Barry Bonds had just hit a grand slam with two outs in the bottom of the ninth to win the seventh game of the World Series. It was absolutely exhilarating!

What better way to send a person off to heaven than slapping high-fives, clapping and hollering praises to the Lord? I wouldn't have been surprised if the dead person had gotten up out of his casket and blessed us with a quick *moonwalk* around the sanctuary. I'm not kidding… it was a party! Too bad most of us will never get to experience that. It's almost like black people "party" into heaven while white people "sneak" into heaven. C'mon folks, if I'm about to enter the Pearly Gates, I want one heck of a party! And if a new believer or seeker observes this type of celebration, they have got to think to themselves: "Hey, this Christianity thing is not only the right thing to do; it's an exciting thing to do!"

Another major league advantage of a mixed ethnicity church is the opportunity to learn about a whole new culture. I'll put my relationship with some of my soul sisters up against any history book in the world. I remember the first time I gave Miss Emma half of a smoked ham. A few weeks later I was visiting her home and noticed a bleached out ham bone hanging above the inside door jam, much the way in which you would hang mistletoe. When I asked her about the significance of this, she explained that when someone gives you a gift of meat, the bone is hung above the door to show appreciation. In addition, an old custom passed down from Miss Emma's mother was that if you placed the bone above the door; God would always provide meat for your home. Show me that in some history book—it ain't gonna happen!

And thirdly, let's assume for a moment we are a seeker or new Christian and just beginning to consider a spiritual life. Personally, I think I would be far more comfortable walking into a full-blown European soccer riot than into some all-white Christian churches. Think of it this way: we are a Republican walking into a room full of Democrats...or vice versa. Can you say, *uncomfortable*? Can you say, *apprehensive*? Can you say, *not going to happen*? And to take it a step further, to some, a one-ethnicity church may project a non-welcoming club or clique-type atmosphere.

Let's consider two scenarios: In both situations we will assume we are exploring Christianity and are now in the process of looking for a church to further our research. We must keep in mind that the church we are about to enter could be the most God-fearing, Bible-teaching, Spirit-filled church in the world, but if the members of this church don't make us feel comfortable, there is a good chance we will never return.

As we enter the first church, we hear various conversations going on. Over near the organ a black lady is addressing a group of several white young ladies. In fact, one black lady (our very own Dee Adams) is overheard joking with some of the choir members and explaining, "Yes, it seems I'm one of the raisins in the Forest Park rice pudding." And as we look around, there are several African-Americans chit-chatting among themselves and with their white counterparts.

Subconsciously we begin to feel at ease, as racial barriers seem to be non-existent in this sanctuary. A lot of that credit goes to our senior pastor, Dr. John Friedman. As a former associate pastor once put it: "Dr. John is as loving as they come." He doesn't see black or white; he just sees souls. And thanks to him, a non-judgmental attitude prevails throughout this congregation.

A black man approaches and welcomes us. Interesting, here he is in a predominately white church but he acts as if this is his church. Wow! Maybe this *is* his church...maybe everyone in this room feels like this is his or her church. How refreshing! However, we are a little surprised. No, we are a lot surprised. We feel totally comfortable...blacks greeting blacks, blacks greeting whites, whites greeting whites, white greeting blacks. "Hey," we think to ourselves, "we might just fit in here." But wait, there's more!

What is this? Miss Emma is dressed to the nines with her swanky new dress and Fifth Avenue hat while talking to Eddie Terry, who is a Louisiana redneck (gotta love Eddie T. and the "Low" Retta Show). Eddie looks like he just got off a boat from Hawaii...flip-flops, bright red/yellow/blue/green shirt and shorts. No way! Way! This church ain't about pretences; it's all about worshiping God. And left at the door you'll find those holier-than-thou attitudes, the fashion show mentality, the racial prejudices and all that other garbage that has absolutely no place in the house of the Lord.

Now for scenario number two: We walk in the second church. Our first question is, "Who died?" We hear very little conversation. We feel like if we speak we'll have to go sit in the corner and write: "I will not talk" twenty-five times on the church blackboard. Lots of white people on Xanax...or so it seems. Some white guy down front dropping pins...we can hear them slam against the floor. What a racket! So quiet we could hear a (you know the saying).

The closest an African-American has ever been to this place is probably the UPS man. Then we make the mistake of sitting in pew number forty, seats five and six. Don't we know that Mr. and Mrs. Johnson own those seats? Of course they do! Mr. Johnson evidently has the tag, title and P.I.N. (Pew Identification Number) in his back pocket. And by the enthusiasm portrayed by this congregation, we might think the average age of this congregation is *deceased*! Everyone is in his or her best Sunday-go-to-meeting clothes. Is today Easter?

Several old ladies are looking at us and pointing...maybe they have never seen a pair of Levi 501 boot cut jeans before.

The preacher begins: "Please acknowledge the existence of the person sitting behind you." A man turns around and looks at us. He turns back around. We suppose our existence has just been acknowledged. We don't know what's next, the prayer, the Pledge of Allegiance or a soldier playing taps, but we know we've had enough. We sum up this "wonderful" experience in just three words: "We're outta here!"

Now, some of us would counter that everyone is welcome in our particular church. But that raises the question: "Have we ever invited a person of color to our church?" If honest, most of us would probably have to say *no*. In fact, if I had been told ten years ago that African-Americans would consider attending, much less joining, our all-white church, I would have vehemently disagreed. And as I have come to find out, I would have been dead wrong! You see folks, it turns out that many times the only thing that stands between us putting a "little raisin in our rice pudding" or a "little rice in our raisin pudding" is the simple invitation. Go figure!

Discussion Guide

1.   As this chapter mentions, it has been said many times that "eleven o'clock on Sunday morning is the most segregated hour in America." Do you agree? _____ What is your opinion concerning the phenomena?

_____

_____

2.   Case Study: You attend an all-white Protestant church. An African American family moves into your neighborhood and you become friends. At supper one evening, as your black guests are dining with your family, the wife asks you where you attend church. She explains that they are looking for a good church

home. Do you recommend several well-known black churches in the area or do you invite their family to attend your church....or both or neither? Please elaborate:

_____

_____

_____

3.   Do you agree that since God created all people, he would not have an issue with them worshiping together? _____ Why or why not?

_____

_____

_____

4.   Have you ever or would you like to attend a church of an ethnic majority other than your own? _____ Do you think you would enjoy the experience? _____ Why or why not?

_____

_____

_____

If given the opportunity, would you invite someone of the opposite ethnicity to your church? _____ If so, do you think your congregation would welcome them with open arms? _____ Why or why not?

_____

_____

_____

_____

Notes:

Chapter Twenty Three

W. W. J. F?

About four years ago I had to Matthew 5:23 someone in our church. That's what I call it when we are obligated to go to a brother or sister in Christ and resolve an issue that we have with them (or vice versa). Matthew 5:23 basically says if a brother or sister has a grudge against us, that before we leave a gift at the altar, we are supposed to go to that person and work out our differences. Then, and only then are we to return to the altar with our offering. By the way, my Matthew 5:23 record is 0-2 and 1. That's no wins, two losses and one tie. Oh well.

My issue with my sister in Christ was that she was forwarding emails to me that were just plain crude. Ah ha! Has a loophole in the Bible just been exposed? Right there in Ephesians 4:29 it says something to the effect of: "…don't let any unwholesome stuff come out of our mouth." Bingo! My sister in Christ thought she had an out…a loophole of sorts. The trash she was forwarding wasn't coming out of her mouth…it was coming out of her *computer*! Well ain't that a fine howdy ya do?

I can't believe the Apostle Paul did not have the foresight to warn us about forwarding profanity. I'm thinking he must have been a low-tech kind of guy…probably didn't even have a laptop. Go figure! How in the world did history's greatest evangelist think he was going to evangelize the planet if he couldn't *Google Greece* or *MapQuest Babylon*? I just don't get it.

Now some of our readers out there probably think I'm exaggerating, huh? Well, I wish I were. Interestingly enough, just as I began writing this morning I received an email from one of my cousins. He is a professing Christian, but we wouldn't know it from his emails. Actually, that's not fair. I would say a majority of his emails reflect his Christian faith, but unfortunately, a few do not. This morning's email was a cute little story about attitudes. And it was chock full of expletives. Only problem was, they weren't deleted.

I honestly believe that some of us must think God isn't paying attention when we forward profane material via our computers. We must believe that forwarding profanity is not nearly as serious as actually saying it. Hello! Not only is forwarding profanity a sin, I think it's actually more destructive than when it comes out of our mouth. Why? Because instead of one person being exposed to our "not so wonderful Christian witness," it's a different story when we send it out into cyberspace. If we forward it to our friends and they forward it to their friends, sooner or later the entire logged-on world would theoretically be exposed to our irreverent emails.

The book of Ephesians does a good job of warning us about unwholesome language coming out of our mouths. But a verse in the book of James just flat knocks it out of the park! That verse, James 1:26, says in effect: "…if any man is religious but does not watch his own tongue, his religion is useless!" Now

I'm sorry people, but it doesn't matter whether we *say* it or we *send* it, that scripture applies.

And here's another issue I have with *forwarded rubbish.* Why do they send it to me? I don't think I'm going to like my answer but here goes. Maybe it's because they think I enjoy it. And maybe that's because I have never had the courage to tell them I don't. Yep...I'm guilty as charged. You see, half of the problem is me.

I could have put a stop to the practice of friends sending me this trash if I had simply said, "Please don't send vulgar emails to me." Imagine if we all sent everyone on our email list a notice that we are no longer accepting any off-color jokes, forwards, etc. What a witness for Christ that would be! And you know what—all it takes is a little courage.

Do some of us lack the courage to tell our friends to stop forwarding garbage? Do we think it will make us look like a wuss? Do we think it might ruin a friendship? Probably all of this stuff, huh? But regardless, some of us need to put a stop to it and that will take courage. And I'm thinking if God could give David the courage it took to go up against that big ole ugly Goliath dude in the OT, he can surely give us the little thimble full of courage it would take to type a "please stop" note and hit the *send* button. Wow...asking God for a tiny snippet of courage, imagine that!

And now back to my sister in Christ, the profanity-forwarding mama! When I first started explaining to her that I felt she was emailing trash, she was offended. Then she went into the denial mode. Next she tried the old "it depends on what your definition of *is* is" excuse. Wow! She had elevated our conversation to the next level...it was almost *presidential,* if you know what I mean. I could tell I was getting nowhere fast...so it was time. Yes, it was time to pull out the dreaded f-bomb. I hate even *thinking* the word, much less *saying* it. But it had to be done; it was the only way to get through her thick skull. By the way, I am an expert on thick skulls; mine was 7.5 inches of solid bone until Jesus showed up in the late Nineties.

Anyway, we were sitting in McDonald's and just when she least expected it; I opened my brief case and pulled out one of the emails she had forwarded to me. I began to read it in a rather loud voice…and yes, it included the f-word.

It was a knee-jerk reaction as she barked, "Shhhh! People can hear you from here to the parking lot!"

"Yes," I smiled, "and when you send out those emails people can read you from here to Afghanistan."

She just sat there…blank stare and all. Then it finally registered. She realized that what I had just done was completely staged. She was embarrassed. Better yet, she was finished, finished sending out profane emails. In fact, she sent me an email the next morning that would become the title of this chapter.

So the next time we might be tempted to forward an email of questionable content, let's just ask ourselves the same question my sister in Christ now asks herself…W.W.J.F?

What Would Jesus Forward?

Discussion Guide

1.   Do you have a friend that occasionally forwards you off-color emails? _____ If so have you ever confronted them about this practice? _____ If you have, please share how you did it and their response.

_____

_____

2.   Why do you think some Christians forward vulgar or off-color emails?

_____

_____

3.   Assuming you are in a new relationship with a Christian brother or sister and they forward you emails of questionable content, should you just ignore it for the time being until you get to know the person better? _____ Why or why not?

_____

_____

_____

4.   Have you noticed that some Christians also tend to forward emails that have a racial overtone to them? _____ If so, we often tend to let things slide. In your opinion, how should we handle such situations?

_____

_____

_____

5.   Do you agree that sending out profane, risqué or emails with racial overtones over the internet can be worse than doing or saying such things in person? _____ Why or why not?

_____

_____

_____

Notes:

Chapter
Twenty
Four

Please Keep Me
in Your Prayers

Here Mary was, thanking me for keeping her family in my prayers. There was only one tiny little problem. I had no earthly idea what she was talking about. Wait! Now I remember! Last week after church as we were leaving, Mary E. and her husband, Mike, approached my car and told me about the upcoming wedding. Evidently there were some serious issues that could possibly come bubbling to the surface as the two families got together. Mary then asked me to keep the entire situation in my prayers. The first thing I did was gladly agree to do so. The second thing I did was to completely forget the conversation ever took place. Hey, it was lunchtime and I was a new and hungry member of the Sunday herd.

So now what do I do? Here she was thanking me for praying for her family while one of her friends, who obviously did not want to be at church, was listening to our conversation. The good news was that evidently, someone's prayers were answered. And other than the three or four fistfights, the wedding ceremony went off without a hitch. I'm thinking one of the Hatfield girls must have married one of the McCoy boys...but that's another story.

So, should I admit that I forgot to pray? How would that sit with Mary's friend, a young lady that was real hesitant about this church thing in the first place? Mary asked me to pray, prayers were answered and now here I was about to admit that I didn't pray at all? What kind of message would that send to Mary's friend? I can just hear her now: "What? A prayer is answered and no one prayed? I should have known all this Christian stuff was bogus!" Mary's visitor might have just found the excuse she needed x-out this whole deal.

Or do I just say, "You're welcome," and let it go at that? Hmmm. Looks like I've got myself between a rock and a hard place. I can either admit I didn't pray, thus giving Mary's friend more ammunition to use against the Christian faith, or I can lie and give God more ammunition to use when he is planning my eternal future. I didn't like either choice!

Here's a novel ideal...the next time I commit to praying for someone, why don't I just go ahead and do it? And I mean right then and there! If I believe in God, I mean *really* believe in God, how can I possibly pass up an opportunity to talk to him even if I'm not coming to him with my own personal "dream sheet." I think most of us would agree that there is nothing more selfless than a prayer for others.

If we think about it, when someone asks us to pray for him or her, we're getting an incredible invitation! An invitation to talk directly to God, the creator of the universe! How can we possibly blow off something as important as that? Okay, it's fess up time. I don't know about our readers, but I do it every day. Yes, I've finally figured out what I have suspected all along; this book is more for my benefit than anyone else's. And just think...if I had actually prayed for Mary's family like I promised, two things may have happened. First, her friend might have been divinely touched when she saw the joy in my eyes as Mary explained to me that my prayers had been answered. And secondly, even the most uninterested observer can't help but notice when the Holy Spirit shows up.

A friend of mine is constantly reminding me that "when God shows up, he shows out!" And when I hear that God has answered one of my prayers, I usually get a serious set of chill bumps. Is that the manifestation of the Holy Spirit? I wouldn't be surprised! And I'm thinking that Mary's friend, *Miss Church, Ain't For Me*, would be asking herself, "What the heck just happened here?" Or if she were really touched, maybe she would be asking herself, "What the heaven just happened here?"

Finally, maybe it's just me but when people ask me to "keep them" in my prayers, I often think to myself: "I don't need to *keep* you in my prayers; I need to *put* you there in the first place." In other words, a lot of people evidently think I'm already praying for them...and I'm not. I should be ashamed of myself, and now that the whole world knows about it, I am. Sorry, my friends, I promise to do better.

Discussion Guide

1.   How many times during the last several weeks has someone asked you to "*keep them in your prayers?*" _____ When someone asks that, do you think that more than likely, they assume you are already praying for them? _____ If being totally honest, how many times would you have to admit, "*Uh, sorry, you're not in my prayers, I forgot to pray for you?*" _____ Do you agree that often times we Christians tell someone we will pray for them and then forget all about it? _____ If you agree, why do you think that is?

_____

_____

_____

Could it be that some of us don't take prayer as serious as we should? _____

2.   Have you ever said, or heard someone say, *"Well, I'd like to help but all I can do is pray about it?"* _____ How might that sound to a non-believer? _____

For instance, what would it sound like if you asked your rich uncle to borrow a million dollars and he responded by saying, *"Well, I'd like to help but all I can give you is twenty-five cents?"* Do you agree when we say something like that it almost sounds like we're scraping the bottom of the barrel? _____ I heard an evangelist on television recently say, *"At least we will be praying for you."* Hello! That's the LEAST he could do? No, I think that's the <u>MOST</u> he could do! Please share your thoughts on this subject:

_____

_____

_____

3.   How many times have you been asked to pray for someone or something and then never informed of the results? _____ Isn't that a little frustrating? _____ Do you agree that we as Christians ought to make some sort of a pact or agreement to let each other know when a prayer has been answered? _____ Okay, raise your right hand, I promise...

Notes:

Chapter Twenty Five

"Saint Act" verses "Sinner Act"

So we are sitting by the water cooler and happen to overhear Tom telling Randy what an incredible worship experience he had at church yesterday. Tom also prays about an issue Randy has. Then Bill walks up and Randy excuses himself and returns to his office. Tom then asks Bill, "So, how did you like the (expletive deleted) that the Yankees put on the Phillies last night? Stomped the (expletive deleted) out of them, huh?" We think to our self, "Hmmm, is that the same Tom that was just praying and bragging about his wonderful church experience a few minutes ago?"

The above scenario started me thinking about my own situation. Do I alter my behavior and my language based on the individual I am with or where I am at the time? I decided to take a personal inventory. The results were mixed. With some people

I am fairly consistent, but with others I am all over the chart, one minute living the exemplary Christian life, the next minute reverting back to my days as a major-league scumbag. And the interesting thing is that my actions are directly related to the person I am with at the time.

For instance, I would not dare say to Sally what I would say to Eric. And although my conversation with Eric might be a touch on the risqué side, it can't hold a candle to what Tim and I might discuss. But hey, Tim is not saved so I can talk to him anyway I want to. I dearly hope our readers all yelled, "No way!" when you read my last sentence. I was just seeing if you were paying attention. Most of you were (smiley face goes here).

I would assume we have all experienced the above scenario to one degree or another. Here is a perfect example: our friend Bart sounds like a real "potty mouth" when we are around him, but let the preacher walk up and all of a sudden we have "Saint Bart." He wouldn't use profanity if his life depended on it. How many of us are like Bart? Some of us may have a "sinner act" and a "saint act," depending on whom we are with at the time.

There are only two words that pose a problem with us having a couple of different "acts." Those words happen to be "Jesus" and "Christ." If we believed in the presence of Jesus as much as we do the presence of the person standing next to us, I suggest many of us would behave totally different. But since we can't see Jesus standing there, it's like we totally ignore his presence. Hello! If we honest-to-God believe Jesus exists, we should know beyond a shadow of a doubt that he is *always* standing next to us!

And here's another problem and what this book is all about. What does it say to the lost and un-churched when we constantly change our behavior patterns depending on whom we are with or where we are at the time? For one thing, it says we aren't consistent. Doesn't the Bible say that Jesus is the same yesterday, today and forever? Unless it was a typo, I think we will find that verse somewhere in the book of Hebrews. And wasn't Jesus supposed to be a role model for us to follow? If he is consistent, aren't we also supposed to display that same trait? But oh, how soon and conveniently some of us forget. Shame on us!

I end this chapter with a rather hard question; at least for me it's hard. Are a few of us deceived? Are a lot of us deceived? Are we really Christians...or is our life just one big act? Can we say that some of us probably deserve an Academy Award? I remember asking a similar question to over one hundred pastors as I went about getting the Cross Reference ready to publish. For those who don't recall, the Cross Reference is my day job. It is a Christian business directory that features local believers in business.

Anyway, my job brought me into contact with a lot of the clergy, and I would typically end our conversation by asking them this question: "How many of the members of your congregation do you think are actually saved?" As we would expect, some wouldn't venture an opinion and those that did usually qualified their answers by saying that it would only be a guess because they could not see into the hearts of the people in their congregations. With that being said, the average response was a mere *thirty percent.* Folks, I don't know about you, but that answer sends chills up and down my spine. If that average is anywhere near accurate, it suggests approximately *seventy percent* of us churchgoers may not be saved.

Can we, as a body of believers, really be that deceived? Maybe the question should be: "If Jesus is supposedly standing right next to us and we gossip or use profanity in our casual conversation, do we really believe he is there in the first place?" Perhaps it may be time for some of us to take a real hard look at our relationship with Christ. About five years ago, I re-examined my relationship and did not like at all what I discovered. All I can do is thank God for his patience and grace, or this boy would still be in that proverbial hand-basket headed south!

I had a friend read this chapter before sending it to press and he had some input. His suggestion was that every time we are having a conversation with someone, we should pretend Jesus is standing right next to us. I explained to him that if we really believed in Jesus Christ, we wouldn't have to pretend. Jesus would in fact, be there. He then countered with, "Okay, if that's the case and we want to cuss or gossip or whatever, I guess we will just have to pretend Jesus is **not** standing there." Bingo! My friend finally got it!

Discussion Guide

1. Some of us Christians may be guilty of changing our behavior patterns depending on whom we are with at the time. For instance, when Kathy and I get together, our conversation invariably ends up concerning church, Bible study or whatever things are pure and noble. But when it's Ralph and I, watch out! Let's just say there's a little mental dumpster diving going on, if you know what I mean. Why do you think some of us alter our behavior like that?

_____

_____

_____

2. Can you recall a time when you have been guilty of altering your behavior to fit the situation or personality of the person you were with at the time? _____ Would you like to share an example with the group? If I were you, I would cough, stammer and go directly to the next question, but for those of you brave enough, feel free.

_____

_____

_____

3. How could this type of behavior affect the way a seeker or non-believer views Christianity?

_____

Do you think they may just be looking for an excuse to blow off Christianity, or do they have a legitimate concern here?

4.   A silent question, no answer necessary. Look around the room. Are there two or more people in this group that might get totally different behavior patterns from you?

5.   How might we as Christians alter our behavior depending on whom we are with at the time? Please give some examples:

Notes:

Chapter Twenty Six

"He's in a Better Place"

How many times have we heard a friend or family member say after someone dies that he or she is in a *better place*? I've heard that more times than I care to remember. Why? Because, if you're like me, on some occasions we've probably had suspicions that he or she may not be in a *better place*... but rather a *hotter place*.

Now don't get me wrong; I fully realize that no one knows an individual's eternal destination except God. But the Bible does give us clues. For instance, the New Testament tells us that we should be able to recognize a child of God by the fruit they bear. So when a person dies that hasn't shown any fruit, are they really headed to heaven? It's very possible, but is it probable? Who knows, right?

The person in question could have been a closet saint...a person with a world-class relationship with Jesus. Yes, typically we will see the fruit, but not necessarily. Imagine this scenario: Ralph (our deceased guy) might have had a very close, yet private relationship with Christ. For instance, maybe he had been spending thousands of dollars to help fight starvation in Africa without anyone, but he and Jesus, knowing what he was doing. Much to everyone's surprise, Ralph could have been a wonderful Christian! The point is that it can be dangerous to judge a book by its cover or a person by his or her ostensible walk with God. But by the same token, we must not take it upon ourselves to give the deceased a free pass to heaven just because we want to make everyone feel good. That is God's call, not ours.

But what about when someone offers up his or her opinion that so-in-so is "in a better place?" Some of us may think: "Hey, what can that hurt? Maybe he or she is *not* in a better place, but there's no harm in being positive." But let's hold our horses—we may have two potential problems with the above scenario. First, what if someone in the secular world, who happens to be a friend, hears us say that Ralph has gone to be with the Lord, but they have some serious doubts or evidence to make them think otherwise? Would it not be easy for this person to rationalize: "Well, if they say Ralph went to heaven, surely I will? After all, I'm a much better person than he was." I know! I know! Being a better person doesn't get us anywhere in the kingdom of God, but that is how a lot of the secular world thinks. And if our main purpose here on earth is to reach out to the lost, sometimes we are going to have to think or rationalize like they do.

Secondly, the comment that Ralph is "in a better place" might cause the friend to write off Christianity as just *organized wishful thinking*. We might hear something like: "Hey, you guys are living in fantasy land and I want no part of it!"

And finally, here's another biggie…what are the eternal consequences when a member of the clergy indicates from the pulpit that so-and-so has passed and gone on to be with the Lord? Well, that depends. If a truly righteous person dies, there isn't an issue. But what about the funeral service in which someone's eternal destination is at best, questionable? Can the presiding member of the clergy risk saying that the deceased has gone to heaven if there is little evidence to support such a conclusion?

This has to be one of the most difficult sermons a pastor ever delivers. What will he or she say during the service about the person that has passed away? Fortunately, most pastors that I know will place life and death significance to this issue. I am positive a vast majority of the clergy takes it to heart when their choice of words in this situation could possibly affect the eternal destinations of some of the attendees. In other words, the consequences of what they say are *huge*!

Likewise, just as with the clergy, we as lay people also need to understand the incredible implications of our comments regarding the deceased. Imagine standing there on Judgment Day as Jesus searches for but can't find an individual's name (let's call him Ricky) in the Book of Life? Then that person looks over at us or in this case *me*, and says: "But, Bobby, I counted on what you told me. After Ricky died, you told me that he had gone on to a better place. After that, I didn't really worry about my spiritual life because I figured if Ricky got into heaven, anybody could." Talk about having blood on my hands! No thanks folks, I pray that never happens to any of us.

Discussion Guide

1.   In the past few years, how many times have you heard the phrase, *"He or she is in a better place?"* _____ Have you ever wondered if in fact, that particular person was in a better place (heaven)?

---

2.   If you have heard the above phrase and were ever concerned whether or not it was true, without naming names and only if comfortable doing so, please share the circumstances surrounding the situation:

---

3.   In your opinion, do you think that saying that the deceased in now in a *"better place"* is a very profound statement and should never be spoken off-handedly? _____ If so please elaborate:

_____

_____

4.   Do you believe that the phrase in question has the potential of having substantial and far-reaching effects, especially if heard by a non-believer if he or she has serious reservations about the party in question? _____ If so, how might that affect the non-believer?

_____

_____

5.   There is a flip side to this issue which is—the family of the deceased may have a much easier time dealing with their loss if they have the hope of eternal life, even if in fact, heaven is not the ultimate destination. What is your opinion concerning this dilemma?

_____

_____

6.   Homework time: Have someone in your group call your pastor and ask his or her take on a funeral where the deceased's salvation is questionable. Share his or her input next week.

Notes:

Chapter Twenty Seven

The Last One

Recently I saw a slogan below someone's email address that said something to the effect of: "For those of you that think it can't be done, please stay out of my way while I'm doing it." That reminded me of my late sister-in-law, Leslie Medlock of Daleville, Alabama. While I can always find a whole boatload of excuses to not witness to a guy just twelve miles across town, Leslie, at the drop of a hat, would travel 12,000 miles across the globe to tell someone about Jesus. Knowing me, I would have just sent an email. Let it suffice to say that if someday a little Chinaman comes up to you in heaven and offers you a delicious entrée of Peking duck… you can thank my sister-in-law.

Why did she go to China to witness for Christ? That's easy… she was looking for one of the "last ones." And because of that, if God has favorites, I'm thinking Leslie is somewhere in the Top Five. In fact, after Mother Teresa, she might have even locked up the *number two spot.*

Here in Panama City, Florida, we have a swimming pool company by the name of Cox Pools. You may have heard of the celebrity sit-com star, Courtney Cox. She is the sister of Richard Cox, the owner. The unique thing about Cox Pools is that over the course of the last few years, many of their employees have come to know Christ. Can you imagine a bunch of roughneck contractors and laborers standing out in the chilly morning air before work singing and praising Jesus? Me neither, but it happens.

Now here's the interesting thing... there is a guy at Cox Pools that everyone refers to as "the last one." He is supposedly one of the last ones at the company that has yet to accept Christ. But guess what? If a couple of guys like Mike Seamon and George Stewart have anything to do with it, the "last one" is just a CWH (Christian Waiting to Happen). I mean c'mon, they won't even let him pour himself a cup of coffee without witnessing to him: "You want cream, sugar and Jesus with that?" Don't believe me? Keep reading.

Mike and George are blue collar Christians and friends of mine. In case any of our readers are not familiar with the term, blue collar Christians don't just talk about witnessing to others, they go out and "get 'er done." There are two types of people in our churches, those that talk *about* the lost and those that talk *to* the lost. Mike and George are talk "to the lost" kind of guys. And believe me, they don't cut their "last one" any slack.

Oh, by the way, our Christian waiting to happen is Rick Medeiros. Rick said I could use his name in this article if I would take him to lunch without witnessing to him. Rick says he's up to about 135 WPD (135 Witnesses Per Day) and it's wearing him out. So naturally I agreed. I also lied, but that's another story. Now, I'm not sure what all goes on at Cox Pools during a typical day, but it sure is fun to imagine. For instance, I'm sure Mike has spilled scalding hot coffee on Rick numerous times and just passed it off as "free little samples from hell." Hmmm, now there's an interesting concept. I wonder what a cup of boiling Folgers would do for my cousin?

And then there's George. I must try to explain him to our readers. When George opens his mouth, even *he* stands back in amazement to hear what he is about to say. Seriously, the boy has no clue what is about to come out of his mouth. The story goes that he once invited Rick to visit his church to observe their *4th Annual Hog-tie a Hypocrite Day*. And believe it or not, Rick was almost ready to accept until he found out they didn't serve popcorn.

Hey! There's a novel idea, why don't churches offer popcorn? Since movie theaters, as we all know, charge about fifty cents per kernel, I'm thinking churches could take a chunk out of the moviegoer market share. And besides, tithing is a lot cheaper than giving up a kidney…isn't that about what it costs to go to a movie these days? The point is that Mike and George will do anything and everything to convince Rick to give Christ a shot. And you know what, I think it's about to happen. When it does, I'm pretty sure we will hear something like the following come out of George's mouth: "Hey Moses, Saint Paul, and Saint Peter…you guys better stand back and take a photograph because heaven is about to throw one heck of a party!"

But let's take this story to the next level. Let's imagine that we have decided to take a mission trip to find *our* last one. We board a plane at the local airport, change planes in Atlanta (that was a no-brainer, huh?) and then we head to South America. We arrive and head immediately deep into the Amazon Rain Forest.

Our vision started nine years ago when we first read of this tribe and the fact that it was located in one of the most remote regions of the world. We read that they were pagans and it was likely they had never been exposed to Christianity. Never in our wildest dreams did we think God would have us come here. But he laid it on our heart years ago and we had never been able to get the thought out of our mind. It was a mission trip ordained by God. And three thousand miles later, here we are witnessing to a young Permon Indian.

Our newfound friend, Kcir, indicates that, yes, he is ready to accept Christ. We ask him and our translator to bow their heads as we began to pray. "Father God, your word says that if we believe that Christ died for our sins, and if we repent, we will be saved. Today Kcir would like to take you up on this incredible offer. Kcir, please repeat after me...Dear God, I am a sinner. I know that Jesus Christ died for my sins. I now repent of my sins and ask Jesus come into my heart and become my Lord and my Savior. Father God, I ask this in the name of your precious son, Jesus Christ."

What was that! What's happening? Oh my God! It can't be! That sound, that blaring sound...a distant trumpet sound, it's getting louder, it's almost deafening. The heavens...they can't be opening! We're scared! We're amazed! We fall to our knees, this is it...it can't be! It must be! "Oh my God, my precious God, you've come back!"

Then it occurs to us! We didn't lead just anyone to the Lord. We, with the help of the Holy Spirit, led the last one...the *very last one*! We can't imagine! We just stepped into history, an honor only one person in the entire world will receive...the ultimate reward for obedience! Talk about a party in heaven; right about now they are having one of "biblical proportions!" Hallelujah!

Ok, back to reality. As all of us know, the above account was fictional... the product of my imagination. But here's the bottom line and the flat truth about the "*very last one*." Someday, someone will in fact, have the greatest privilege ever bestowed on mankind...the honor of having God use him or her to bring his last child home. And guess what, that person could be you! If you bought this book, God knows you're trying to become more like Him and less like you...and I'm thinking that's the kind of person that God will choose to help him wrap things up here on earth.

Thanks for buying this book. I hope you enjoyed reading it as much as I did writing it. God bless…see ya in heaven!

P.S.   As you may recall, the last one's name in our fictional account was Kcir. I wonder what that spells backwards? Could it be? Hmmm…

Discussion Guide

We thought our last chapter discussion should be a review. We sincerely pray you enjoyed this book and maybe even got something out of it. May God richly bless each and every one of you. Okay, let's get to it:

1.   What is the number one thing you took away from this book (assuming you did get something out of it)?

_____

_____

_____

2.   In your opinion, what is the most effective way to witness? Is it verbal, is it by example, or a combination of the two? _____ Please elaborate:

_____

_____

_____

3.   If you have reservations or fear about witnessing verbally, do you think writing a letter to the person might be a good way to open a witnessing experience? _____ Why or why not?

_____

_____

_____

_____

4.   If you agree with the premise of this book, what would you say is the number one way we alienate other individuals from the Christian faith?

_____

_____

_____

5.   If a person were to tell you the reason he or she shuns the Christian faith is because there aren't enough *red headed preachers*, should you take him or her seriously? _____ Why or why not?

_____

_____

_____

6.   Case Study: You have a dear friend who is a wonderful Christian. Unfortunately, he is a terrible driver and yes, he has all kinds of Christian bumper stickers on his vehicle. Should you say something to him about that? _____ If so, what is a tactful way to approach such an issue?

_____

_____

_____

_____

_____

Notes:

Chapter Twenty Eight

The Invitation
How Long is Eternity?
Where Will We Spend It?

Have you ever wondered how long eternity is? Well, let me try to put it into perspective. Imagine that once every 10,000 years a small sparrow flies down from the North Pole to Panama City Beach in Florida. When he arrives, he picks one grain of sand off the beach and flies it back to the North Pole. After another 10,000 years, he returns down to Panama City Beach and picks up yet another grain of sand...and flies it back to the North Pole. So, how long is eternity? Well, when that little sparrow, who only comes once every 10,000 years for a single grain, when he has finished taking every single grain of sand off the sixteen miles of Panama City Beach... that represents less than one tenth of one second of time in eternity!

But The Good News Is…You Can Accept Jesus Right Here and Right Now…and spend eternity in Heaven with Him. Just say this simple prayer: Dear Father, I'm at the end of my rope! I've tried to live my way and realize that I can't go one more day without you in my life. I ask your forgiveness for my sins. I thank you and trust that you will forgive me…not because of anything I have done to deserve it, but because Jesus, who is God Himself, died for my imperfections. Father, I look forward to having a relationship with you and allowing you to be the Lord of my life. Please accept me as I am…but don't let me stay this way. Guide me and change me to be like your Son. Amen.

Congratulations! If you prayed the above prayer with a sincere heart, you have just caused a party in heaven! Read Luke, Chapter 15, Verse 7 which says something to the effect of: "…*there will be more celebration in heaven over one sinner who repents than over ninety-nine who need no repentance.*"

God Bless You and Keep You!

bobby weaver